A CROSS CULTURAL ENCOUNTER: A NON-TRADITIONAL APPROACH TO SOCIAL WORK EDUCATION

FLORENCE SCHWARTZ, FRITZ A. FLUCKIGER AND IRVING WEISMAN

5.55

San Francisco, California
1977

Published By

R AND E RESEARCH ASSOCIATES
4843 Mission Street, San Francisco 94112
18581 McFarland Avenue, Saratoga, California 95070

Publishers

Robert D. Reed and Adam S. Eterovich

Library of Congress Card Catalog Number

76-56471

ISBN

0-88247-449-9

PREFACE

This monograph was financed in part by the National Institute of Drug Abuse (NIDA) of the Alcohol, Drug Abuse, Mental Health Administration (ADAMHA). It deals with a program that involved two components: study of Puerto Rican culture and study of drug abuse. The two components were dealt with separately as well as in relation to each other. The project originally involved an exchange of students between the University of Puerto Rico School of Social Work and the Hunter College School of Social Work. The initial emphasis was placed on learning the language and culture through field work experience in drug agencies in Puerto Rico for the New York students and in New York for the Puerto Rican students. After the first year, the model was changed because of administrative complications and learning needs, eliminating the student exchange. Hunter College School of Social Work graduate students spent a period of time in Puerto Rico for training in language and culture, utilizing several unique facilities and approaches.

In this document, we focus on the cross cultural experience as a special characteristic of the project in preparing students to function in a bilingual world, an area where little has been done in social work training. The efforts to prepare primarily Anglo students to speak Spanish and to relate to the culture of a large part of the New York City population provided many benefits for the students, for the faculty involved, for the program of the Hunter College School of Social Work, and for the participating agencies. Hopefully it will benefit some of the people being served by graduates of the program.

It took the efforts of many people to make the three project cycles work:

Eleanor Carroll, the National Institute of Drug Abuse project officer, who encouraged the exploration of the impact of drug abuse on members of the Hispanic community, and James Callahan, project officer, who supported training efforts;

Margaret Daniel and Dr. Milton Wittman of the Social Work Training Branch of the National Institute of Mental Health who sought to broaden the quality of social work education;

Dr. Ruth G. Weintraub, former Dean of the Social Sciences Division of Hunter College, who supported the development of the program in its early stages;

Dr. Ernest Bergauer, Director of the Research Administration Office, Hunter College;

Dean Harold Lewis of the Hunter College School of Social Work;

Ms. Yolanda Mayo, project staff member, field instructor, interpreter of Hispanic culture to staff and students, whose entire family became involved in the program, who contributed beyond the call of duty;

The Hunter College School of Social Work Field Office, which participated in locating field agencies that dare to change the model by accepting students for placement in January;

The Bernstein Institute, Jack Pinsen and Wini Norman, in particular; Greenwich House, Anita Kurman, Director;

Dean Rosa Marin and the faculty of the University of Puerto Rico Graduate School of Social Work who gave generously of their time and interest;

The entire staff of the Puerto Rico Learning Center in Ponce;

The Secretary of the Department of Social Services of the Commonwealth of Puerto Rico, who provided support and encouragement;

The many people in the Puerto Rican community and the professionals in the drug (treatment) community who contributed their knowledge and skill;

The faculty members of Catholic University of Ponce;

The Advisory Committee and the project staff; and

Cyrille Weisman and Martin Schwartz whose active interest, suggestions and valuable assistance during the entire project period were most welcomed and appreciated.

Last, but not least, the three groups of students who made this project live.

Florence S. Schwartz
Fritz A. Fluckiger
Irving Weisman

HUNTER COLLEGE SCHOOL OF SOCIAL WORK

Dr. Irving Weisman   Project Director

Dr. Florence S. Schwartz   Curriculum Associate

Dr. Fritz A. Fluckiger   Research Associate

Ms. Yolanda Q. Mayo   Field Instructor

Ms. Rachel Singer   Administrative Assistant

UNIVERSITY OF PUERTO RICO SCHOOL OF SOCIAL WORK 1971

Dr. Rosa Marin   Dean

Dr. Belen Serra   Coordinator of Academic Affairs

Professor Luz A. Munoz   Field Placement Office

Professor Juanita Carrillo   Curriculum Associate

Dr. Adriana Guzman   Research Associate

Mrs. Dimna de De Choudens   Field Instructor

PUERTO RICO LEARNING CENTER 1972/1973

Dr. Raymond Smith   Director

Al Woolston   Deputy Director of Training

Al Ferraro   Deputy Director of Administration

Angel Maldonado   Coordinator of Spanish Language
                                     Training

William Stillwell   Program Advisor, 1972

Jean Abinader   Program Advisor, 1973

MEMBERS OF THE ADVISORY COMMITTEE

Elsa Arcelay
Addiction Services Agency
New York, New York 10013

Jesse T. Arnette
Associate Commissioner
New York State
Drug Abuse Control Commission
New York, New York 10048

Dr. Larry A. Bear
Consultant on Drug Abuse
Health Insurance Plan
New York, New York 10033

Roy Y. Eng
Senior Consultant
New York City Department
   of Mental Health and Mental
   Retardation Services
New York, New York 10013

Yolanda Q. Mayo
Hunter College School of
   Social Work
New York, New York 10021

Lillian C. Lampkin
Associate Dean
Hunter College School of
   Social Work
New York, New York 10021

Ritz Ortiz
Assistant Professor
Columbia University School
   of Social Work
New York, New York 10026

Dr. Trina Rios
Associate Professor
Herbert H. Lehman College
Bronx, New York 10468

J. Julian Rivera
Associate Professor
Adelphi University
Garden City, New York 11350

Dr. Vera Rubin
Research Institute for the Study
   of Man
New York, New York 10021

Luis Samuel
Director
Fulton Community Based Center
Bronx, New York 10457

Mrs. Evelyn Stiefel
Psychiatric Social Worker
New York, New York 10021

Carmen Torres
Center for International Education
Queens College
Flushing, New York 11367

Dr. Carmen Rivera de Alvarado
Professor
Hunter College School of
   Social Work
New York, New York 10021

STUDENT PARTICIPANTS IN THE PROJECT

CYCLE ONE

Maryellen Benedetto
Ted Butler
Harvey Chasser
Betty Crosby
Paul Kaiser
Charlene Shaffer
Roberta Todras
Carole Weiser

University of Puerto Rico
School of Social Work
Students in Program:

Joseph Brennan
Nilsa Burgos de Canals
Helen Marie Casanova
Ada Iris Oliveras Gonzalez
Elsie Gonzalez Pereyo
Nilsa Rivera Pietri
Sonia Colon Rodriquez
Nilsa Limbert Rodriquez
Edda Torress Vidal

CYCLE TWO

Jean Cutler
George Gallo
Joan Garofalo
Beverly Harris
Minnie Jones
Stanley Lemel
Judith Milone
William O'Connor
Susan Pfannkuche
John Phillips
Ellen Russin
Shelley Solomon
Louise Vargas
Barbara Yeager

CYCLE THREE

Janet Adler-Horton
Linda Ford
Paulette Geanacopoulos
Cynthia Gray-Biggs
Barbara Keller
Pearlie Klutz
Neil McAuliffe
Michael Navas
Martha Schwartz
Barbara Watts

TABLE OF CONTENTS

Page

PREFACE iii

SECTION I   THE BACKGROUND OF THE PROJECT 1

    INTRODUCTION 1

        CHAPTER   1   CONCEPTUAL FRAMEWORK 5
        CHAPTER   2   EDUCATIONAL RATIONALE 19
        CHAPTER   3   SELECTED CENSUS DATA ABOUT PUERTO RICAN POPULATION
                      ON MAINLAND U. S. A. 25
        CHAPTER   4   THE NEW YORK PUERTO RICAN COMMUNITY 30
        CHAPTER   5   PUERTO RICAN LITERATURE 33
        CHAPTER   6   IMMIGRATION AND ASSIMILATION 39
        CHAPTER   7   SOCIAL PROBLEMS AND MENTAL HEALTH 48
        CHAPTER   8   THE CROSS CULTURAL PROJECT WITH PUERTO RICO ... 58
        CHAPTER   9   THE SETTING - PONCE 64

SECTION II   THE EXPERIENCE OF THE STUDENTS:
                      PROBLEMS AND REATIONS 66

    INTRODUCTION 66

        CHAPTER 10   FIRST REACTIONS 69
        CHAPTER 11   LIVING ARRANGEMENTS 81
        CHAPTER 12   COMMUNICATION AND LANGUAGE 86
        CHAPTER 13   EXPERIENCES WITH SELECTED FAMILY BELIEFS, ATTITUDES
                      AND BEHAVIORS 93

                      A.   Education 93
                      B.   Family Roles 97
                      C.   Sex Roles 99
                      D.   Work Roles 106
                      E.   Religion 108

SECTION III   THE OUTCOME OF THE PROJECT 113

    INTRODUCTION 113

        CHAPTER 14   SUMMARY 114
        CHAPTER 15   RECOMMENDATIONS 123

                      BIBLIOGRAPHY 129

THE BACKGROUND OF THE PROJECT

INTRODUCTION

The Hunter College School of Social Work, part of the City University of New York, has a special concern for the problems of the City. For a number of years the School has had special programs aimed at preparing more minority group members to work in the social agencies throughout the City. In part, these are based on the belief that the value orientation of the social worker affects the relationship between client and worker and between agency and society and that it is highly desirable to prepare more minority group members as social workers to serve their communities.

At the end of the 60's, it was becoming increasingly clear that the growing New York Puerto Rican population, relegated to low economic and social position as unskilled, unfamiliar with the language, and facing color barriers, were consumers of a considerably higher proportion of health and welfare services than their 10% of the population might indicate.

Unskilled Puerto Ricans move from their rural homes to San Juan and then to the mainland. "Most migrants are rural people who may have first stopped in a San Juan slum".[1] Not all come planning to stay in New York. Many come with a plan to work, save, return to la isla, buy a home or perhaps start a business. According to Meyers and Masnick's exploratory study, 33.5% of their sample of New York Puerto Ricans said they will definitely return to Puerto Rico.[2] However, in actuality many do stay and though some rise from poverty to middle class, about half live in poverty.

This increase in population called for a mobilization by social work agencies to deal with the special needs of the Puerto Rican client group. However, in many cases, the agencies have been unable to provide effective service. A prime reason for this inability has been the lack of sufficient Spanish-speaking personnel. In addition, there has been resistance by the Puerto Ricans to make use of the social agencies because of the insensitivity of some professionals to the lifestyle and social behavior of Puerto Rican people. Such phenomena as the significance of the Puerto Rican extended family, the role of father and mother in relation to children, the role of spiritualism, and the concepts of machismo and respeto, are frequently not understood by social workers; a social worker's lack of understanding can actually lead to improper treatment because of a misreading of the significance of certain behavior.

One of the special problems is that of drug abuse, an area in which the number of Puerto Ricans known to the Narcotics Register appears to be greater than their proportion of the population.

It has been increasingly evident that attempts to recruit more Spanish-speaking students to graduate social work training produced limited results, since the pool of Hispanics who complete bachelor degrees remains small.

A Cross-Cultural, Cross-Regional Drug Project with Puerto Rico

The "Intervention with Drug Abusers: Cross-Cultural, Cross-Regional" project*

* Project funded by the National Institute of Mental Health, Grant No. DA 00014-03.

began in July 1970. To increase the cadre of professional social work personnel with knowledge of the Hispanic culture, with awareness of life experiences prior to arrival in New York, with ability to relate to both verbal and non-verbal communications, and with speaking knowledge of Spanish, it was decided to take into the project Anglo* students who had completed one year of social work education and attempt to prepare them to work with the Spanish-speaking population. A few third generation Puerto Ricans and Spanish-speaking students who wanted to learn more about the culture from which they came also were included.

The goals of the project were:

1. To enable the student to gain an understanding of the culture and social environment from which the Puerto Rican clients come.

2. To develop the student's language skill to be able to communicate with the Puerto Rican community.

3. To have the student experience the stimulation of living in another culture in order to develop heightened sensitivity and awareness of oneself as a cultural being and to understand the cultural determinants of behavior.

4. To familiarize the student with the problem of drug abuse in Puerto Rico and in New York City.

In long range terms, the goals were:

1. To develop curriculum material that can be incorporated into the overall content of the school.

2. To stimulate greater awareness of the needs of various ethnic groups.

3. To prepare students for practice in the social agencies of New York, with greater relevance to the Puerto Rican population.

4. To contribute to change in student, faculty and agency understanding and attitudes regarding service delivery, particularly regarding drug abuse.[3]

5. To contribute to increased knowledge in the field through research.

During the first year of the project, an attempt was made to prepare the students in Spanish language and culture in New York during the summer prior to their leaving for San Juan, Puerto Rico, where they spent a period of time in field work with drug agencies under the supervision of the faculty of the University of Puerto Rico Graduate School of Social Work.

The second and third year, the project was moved to the Puerto Rico Learning Center of Catholic University in Ponce, Puerto Rico. This is the center used by the Peace Corps in preparing their volunteers for work in the Spanish-speaking countries, and for industrial firms active in Latin America.

Before the students left for Puerto Rico, which was during their third semester of work, three weeks in September were devoted to a full-time program of orientation to Puerto Rico and to problems of drug abuse.

* Anglo here is used to refer to American-born students, white or black, not identified with Spanish-speaking groups.

The orientation period included field trips to <u>la marketa</u>, <u>botanicas</u>, and <u>bodegas</u>, as well as visits to an <u>espiritista</u> and a Pentacostal Church in East Harlem. After the three-week orientation, the students went to Puerto Rico for the following twelve weeks, until mid-December.

The experience in Puerto Rico had three aspects: 1) language trainings; 2) cultural training; and 3) technical training.

The language program was 250+ hours over a twelve week period with a heavier concentration of work during the first few weeks.

The basis for the cultural training was the <u>Barrio</u> Live-in. During the twelve weeks in Puerto Rico each student was assigned to live with a family in a <u>Barrio</u> (neighborhood) or a housing development (urbanization). They were encouraged to participate with their families in family related activities both in the home and in the community.

The work-in phase or technical training of the program in Puerto Rico was related to the development of specific skills needed by the students to perform a job in his/her area of interest. After participant observation, there was opportunity for some direct practice in the last three weeks of their stay.

In addition to the experiential learning, cognitive material was included as part of the facilitation or feedback sessions. This included lectures, discussions, and class sessions at the Catholic University of Ponce dealing with the Puerto Rican family, employment and migration in Puerto Rico, religion and spiritualism, the New York Puerto Rican, problems of culture shock, the social pathology in Puerto Rico. There were also several sessions with the Counseling Educational Department of Catholic University in which the students did cross-cultural interviewing and counseling through role playing and videotaping.

After their return, and after the "debriefing session", the students were assigned to their field work placements, which were planned so that they would be able to use their knowledge of Spanish and culture to work with the Puerto Rican community in a variety of social work agencies with emphasis on the alcohol and drug abuse settings. In addition, the students completed their course work and their research projects as required for graduation.

Footnotes:

1. Joseph G. Fitzpatrick. <u>The Puerto Rican Americans</u>. (Englewood Cliffs, N.J.: Prentice-Hall, 1971), p. 3

2. George C. Meyers and George Masnick. "The Migration Experience of New York Puerto Ricans: A Perspective on Return". <u>International Migration Review</u> (Spring 1968), p. 80 - 90.

3. Irving Weisman. <u>Social Work Intervention with Drug Abusers: Cross-Cultural, Cross-Regional</u>. Project funded by the National Institute of Mental Health, MH 12499. 1970

CHAPTER 1

CONCEPTUAL FRAMEWORK

There is a growing body of material which indicates that various ethnic groups differ in their response to social problems, to health and illness, to personal and interpersonal difficulties, and to family relationships; but there is little material about how the helping professional may use this data.

This monograph describes a program which attempted to train primarily Anglo social workers to work with a particular ethnic group - Puerto Ricans - by introducing them to the culture and language of this group.

Culture has been defined by Kroeber and Kluckhohn as "patterns, explicit and implicit, of and for behavior acquired and transmitted by symbols, constituting the distinctive achievements of human groups....; culture systems may, on the one hand, be considered as products of action, on the other hand as conditioning elements of further action."[1]

These "conditioning elements" are predispositions toward behavior based on a vast and complex network including among other things, values, history, customs and language. The "distinctive achievements" of each human group result in the distinctive behavioral patterns of each group.

Intercultural experience provides the intuitive grounds for accepting as plausible, without systematically collected evidence, the assumption that there are psychological differences of some importance between human populations.[2]

Ralph Kolodony points out that social workers know very little about the meanings that clients and group members attach to differences in custom and ceremonies, value orientations, food habits, language, etc.[3] A similar point is made by Alejandro Garcia.

It is the contention of the Chicano that the white social work practitioner is for the most part ignorant of Chicano culture, values, aspirations, and that this ignorance has contributed significantly to stifling the upward mobility potential of Chicanos in this country. It would appear that the social service agencies have also remained insensitive to the differences between the Chicano culture and the majority culture. Part of the fault of these shortcomings lies with the schools of social work. For too long, the schools of social work have either been blind or indifferent to cultural differences of minority groups, especially Chicanos and Blacks. Only in recent years have they begun to recognize their shortcomings in this curricula.[4]

In many instances clients are considered resistant to receiving help when in reality it may be resistance to acceptance of a worker's alien value system.

The Nature of Cross Cultural Training

The complex character of the training required is indicated by Giordano.

> Ethnicity from a clinical point of view is more than a distinctive-
> ness defined by race, religion, national origin, or geography. It
> involves conscious and unconscious processes that fulfill a deep
> psychological need for security, identity, and a sense of historical
> continuity. It is transmitted in an emotional language within the
> family and is reinforced by similar units in the community.[5]

The pluralistic nature of American society makes the understanding of different cultures even more important.

> The field of inter-cultural communication arose from the need of practition-
ers to cope with and work in a strange culture. The move away from a theory of the
melting pot for the United States to a recognition of the cultural pluralism that
exists within our society calls for a re-examination of the way social workers deal
with differences.

> The myth of the melting pot has obscured the great degree to which
> Americans have historically identified with their national citizen-
> ship through their myriad subnational affiliations. This has meant in-
> evitable competition, friction and conflict.[6]

Recent years have seen the resurgence of the search for group identity, at least in
part, as a response to the new challenges by Blacks and other minority groups. There
appears to be a reassertion of ethnic identification and organization among third and
fourth generations.

What the Social Worker Needs to Know

Social workers need to know what the adaptive capabilities of the individual
are, and how they may be used, as well as the supports in the family, social, ethnic,
work and neighborhood groups. Garcia identifies the social work training areas related
to cross-cultural practice as:

1. Analyzing value systems concepts;
2. Comprehending and valuing the nature and impact of cultural
   heritage;
3. Understanding the influence of lifestyle environments such
   as child rearing patterns, familial associations and psychological sets;
4. Detailing and analyzing differentiations as influenced by
   class, culture, cross-culture and regions.[7]

In order to be effective in responding to different groups, the student needs to inte-
grate cognitive and experiential material. Cross-cultural education can be culture
specific or culture general. General training refers to self-awareness and sensitivity training that allows one to learn about himself and to prepare for interaction
with other cultures. Specific training refers to information about the particular
culture.

> The person undergoing acculturation must first recognize his own style of
behavior, attitudes, beliefs and the personal assumptions that will allow him to experience another culture.

> It is insight into one's own values and assumptions that permits
> growth of a perspective which recognizes that differing sets of
> values and assumptions exist (i.e., cultural relativism) and develop-
> ment of the potential for greater understanding of another culture.[8]

The process of becoming educated in another culture, according to Walsh, involves a broad view:

> Knowledge of the history of a culture and its religious system and orientation supplies the necessary background and one integrating framework for a more detailed study of the culture. In this detailed study, there is practically no branch of knowledge that does not yield rewarding insights. ...The culture expresses itself both in what it does and in what it does not do. What constitutes a culture is the very fact that the people in it experience the real work in their own way; the experience itself is different from any other, and different cultures put varying emphasis on differing aspects of their experience. The study of a culture, therefore includes its psychology, its perceptions of beauty, its regard for people and things, its political and military organization, its cognitive and affective levels, its economic status, and its ethical patterns.[9]

Daniel Sanders offers a similar approach:

> ....the mere provision of one or two courses related to culture, comparative social work minority groups, or Black history, amounts only to tokenism; that instead, a cross-cultural and pluralistic perspective should permeate the entire curriculum.[10]

> With adequate planning and participation from the host country, field projects in other countries....could provide valuable insights and opportunities to be exposed to other cultures and patterns of life.[11]

Another social work educator suggests:

> Special competence would have to be developed in working with ethnic minorities, and religious and cultural groups to understand their aspirations and to help develop policies that would insure greater justice to them. Opportunity should be provided for work with ethnic groups to help understand their traditions, family patterns, cultural symbols and sex and age roles.[12]

Social Values:

It was the assumption of the project faculty that major value themes in Puerto Rican culture were essentially Latin American, and the Latin American values were primarily Spanish in origin. This assumption suggested that it might be a useful exercise to, in fact, identify the specific broader context of Puerto Rican values in Latino values and Spanish values.

The exercise proved to be more complex than anticipated. Gillin notes that:

We have persisted in viewing the Latin Americans either as degenerate Indians struggling with the ruins of a conquest-wrecked native culture or as tainted Iberians fumbling with the traditions of Spain and Portugal. It is as if, since "angel food" cake contains appreciable amounts of sugar and beaten eggs, we should refuse to recognize it as an angel food cake, but insist on considering it either an omelet or a chunk of candy. The general culture of our southern neighbors seems to be neither basically Spanish, Portuguese, or "modern European"- except within the walls of luxury hotels and the boulevards of capital cities.[13]

He comments that Latin America, as distinct from other Western civilizations, has much to do with three centuries of Spanish colonization. Evidence includes the family organization and member roles, ceremonial kinship patterns (godparents, etc.), the concept of personal honor, and the emphasis on inter-personal relations.

> Thus all are nominally Roman Catholic, and many of the details of content and organization are those of Iberian Catholicism as distinguished from the North European type; e.g., cult of the saints, public <u>fiestas</u> and parades, greater development of sodalities (<u>cofraidias</u>, <u>hermanidades</u>, etc.), more emphasis upon monastic orders, and so on. Of course the Spanish language itself with sundry modifications has become a part of Latin American culture. Ideologically this culture is humanistic, rather than puritanical, if such a contrast is permissible. Intellectually, it is characterized by logic and dialectics, rather than by empiricism and pragmatics; the word is valued more highly than the things; the manipulation of symbols (as in argument) is more cultivated than the manipulation of natural forces and objects (as in mechanics). Patterns of medieval and sixteenth century mysticism are strong in the culture, and these patterns show no inconsistency with those of argumentation, for, as with the medieval scholastics, the worth of the logic lies in the manipulation of concepts, not in the empirical investigation of premises.[14]

Examination of social organization in Latin America[15] emphasizes:

1. the <u>compadre</u> ceremonial kinship system which is often complicated and may extend to almost every family in a community. Sponsorship (e.g., godparents) is the mechanism by which the relationship is established; the system offers great security to its members.

2. the stable and extended family group. Having many children is considered a prestige symbol.

3. the maintenance of social status and prestige.

4. the double standard in sex behavior and the division of labor by sex role.

Clearly specifying specific cultural elements transmitted from Spain is not easy. Gillin suggests that the Spanish Crown was restrictive during the colonial period, and did not wish many of the elements of "modernism" in Western Europe to reach the colonies. What did come through seems to be a limited version of Spanish culture, an equivalent of Medieval Europe, and not the "Renaissance" and "Enlightment" which arrived in Spain so late.

> In suggesting areas for additional study, Davidson concludes:

> A thorough analysis of the fifteenth century Spanish culture must be made. The romance historian needs to tell us just what elements were prevalent in fifteenth century Spain and also in the Colonial Period. Only by having this other side of the original elements of the Latin American culture subject to intensive study can we hope to obtain a balanced picture.[16]

Contrasts in Value Orientations

Using sociological and anthropological views, Florence Kluckhohn developed a framework for comparing cultures based upon their implicit and explicit premises about five problems believed to be crucial to all human groups. These premises relate to: the character of human nature; the relation of man to nature (and supernature); the time orientation of human life; the activity orientation; the relationship orientation. The schema rests on the assumption that there are a limited number of common human problems which have variable solutions within a range of possible solutions; that all alternatives are present in all societies at all times but are preferred differentially in rank ordering of dominant and varient patterns. Organized into a table often used by cultural anthropologists these premises appear as follows:

THE FIVE VALUE ORIENTATIONS AND THE RANGE OF VARIATIONS POSTULATED FOR EACH[2]

Orientation	Postulated Range of Variations					
human nature	Evil		Neutral	Mixture of Good-and-Evil	Good	
	mutable	immutable	mutable	immutable	mutable	immutable
man-nature	Subjugation-to-Nature		Harmony-with-Nature		Mastery-over-Nature	
time	Past		Present		Future	
activity	Being		Being-in-Becoming		Doing	
relational	Lineality		Collaterality		Individualism	

[2]The arrangement in columns of sets of orientations is only the accidental result of this particular chart. Although statistically it may prove to be the case that some combinations of orientations will be found more often than others, the assumption is that all combinations are possible ones. For example, it may be found that the combination of first-order choices is that of Individualism, Future, Doing, Mastery-over-Nature, and Evil mutable, now changing, as in the case of the dominant middle-class culture of the United States, or that it is, as in the case of the Navaho Indians, a combination of the first-order preferences of Collaterality, Present, Doing, Harmony-with-Nature, and Good-and-Evil (immutable).   17

Value orientation are described as complex, patterned-rank-ordered-principles arising from the interplay of cognitive, affective and directive elements in the thoughts and acts and feelings involved in the solving of basic human problems.

At the risk of over-simplification, the Kluckhohn system will be used as a tool for identifying some Mainland and Puerto Rican value orientations.

Human Nature Orientation:

Many North Americans believe that human nature is basically evil, but may be improved by control and discipline to a state of goodness. A growing number seem to believe that human nature consists of a mix of good and evil, and that while control is needed, slips can be understood and need not be severely punished.

Puerto Ricans seem inclined to believe that man is not naturally good, and that individuals must be careful lest others trick or exploit them.

Man-Nature (Supernature) Orientation:

The dominant North American view is that man unequivocally must master nature. "God helps those who help themselves." Continents, oceans and space are to be conquered for the benefit of man. The belief is common that technology exploiting nature holds the solutions to all of man's problems. The world is likely to be thought of as consistent and orderly in both nature and the supernatural by Puerto Rican Islanders. While the social world is not thought of as necessarily good, the supernatural world is believed to be good, with gods and spirits enabling man to do good, and not evil. Man is more likely to be subjugated by nature and as a victim of his fate than to be nature's master, which may account for what is often described as a fatalistic attitude.

Time Orientation:

More than most peoples, North Americans look to a bigger and better future in material rather than in social terms. Many are not content with the present, and do not venerate the past merely because it is the past. Future oriented Americans are by no means non-conformists in many areas of life, and in particular in reference to certain "hallowed" beliefs.

Traditions of the past and exigencies of the present have tended to heavily influence Puerto Rican life, although in recent years mainland influences have introduced more of a future orientation.

Activity Orientation:

Characteristically North American is the active "doing" orientation backed by many slogans about getting things done. Individual worth tends to be directly equated with tangible achievement. Problem-solving and learning are defined as active processes. Achieved status is generally valued above ascribed status. The more tradition-bound island culture is likely to place high emphasis on the ascribed social characteristics achieved by birth into a particular family. As noted earlier, Latin cultures tend to value words and concepts and their manipulation more than actions. By most ordinary measures Puerto Ricans are described as passive and accepting. It is recognized that among Puerto Ricans there exist groups which are active, aggressive and initiating in their modes of action, and there seems to be some movement in this direction.

Relational Orientation:

Individuality and equality are strongly emphasized in Mainland child rearing, education and socialization; autonomy and personal responsibility are thought of as desirable for all. This is related to a preference for minimal authority and democratic decision-making rather than strong central leadership.

Central concern for the extended family and ritual kin has made for a collaterally rather than an individually oriented society for Puerto Ricans. Relationships

in barrios and villages are of a gregariousness not necessarily found on the mainland. Individual isolation is thought to be improper. A traditional respect for
authority and dominance differs considerably from the mainland verbalized expectation
of equality.[18]

This general and limited comparison of selected value orientations in accor-
dance with the Kluckhohn system is presented to highlight some of the differences
and not to suggest that either is "better" than the other.

Selected Customs, Traditions, Ideas and Attitudes Which are Part of the Puerto Rican
Social Heritage.[19]

Mintz, in his careful analysis, emphasizes that "national variant values
and behaviors, that dominant forms are by no means universal and probably have different symbolic meaning to different segments of the population, and that national "characteristics" or identities are imputations and not facts. He concludes that genuinely
distinctive Puerto Rican character traits or values are extremely hard to identify or
corroborate by social science methods.

Not inconsistent with the basic family group orientation is the Puerto Rican
concept which emphasizes that the inherent worth and equality of the person accords him
respect regardless of his social position. He has a sense of dignity (dignidad) and
is respected (respeto) as a good man who carries out expected social roles. "Respeto
demands that proper attention be given to culturally prescribed ceremonial rituals
and order that must be observed in interpersonal relationships."[20] Among these rituals
of respect are:

1. Handshaking is expected when encounters begin and end; if people are familiar, they may embrace rather than shake hands. It is also appropriate for a subordi-
nate to offer his hand to one considered his superior. If the offered hand is not taken,
the Puerto Rican feels rejected and affronted. He withdraws and breaks contact (de respeto or no consideraron a uno).

2. Greeting and saying goodbye are formalities for which all persons stand.

3. In all correspondence, including letters to friends or family, formal
greetings and closing are used.

4. On visits to homes, the offering and accepting of food, coffee, cigarettes, etc. is expected. It is a falta de educacion not to offer and a falta de
concideracion not to accept.

5. Deference is expressed to a superior. Ceremonial conduct demands that
the Puerto Rican agree verbally with the authority figure even when he disagrees and
has no intention of acting. This kind of behavior is sometimes defined as "lying"
by Anglos. Under such conditions a Puerto Rican will feel hurt, unjustly accused,
and disrespectfully treated. Puerto Ricans are taught to look down and not to make
eye contact when scolded. This action may be interpreted by North Americans as guilt
and a confirmation of the basis of the reprimand or accusation.

The converse of respeto, relajo, uses an idiom privileged insult which is permissible only among intimates, and never among unequals or acquaintances. Hidalgo notes
that it is not appropriate to make fun of a person's characteristics, and that Puerto
Ricans are not accustomed to laugh at themselves or their shortcomings.[21] Puerto Ricans
do not engage in the defamation games sometimes played by mainland Blacks "jiving" or
"playing the dozens". This may account for the reluctance of many Puerto Ricans referred

to social agencies because of personal problems to participate in groups using confrontation techniques, i. e. group therapy, therapeutic communities which use encounter techniques.

Among Puerto Ricans great sensitivity exists to what is experienced as a personal insult, and a lack of proper respect. The strong responses to a perceived affront may cover the continuum from withdrawal to assaultive violence.

Another consequence of this "personalism" is a view of life as a network of interpersonal relationships, and a reliance on known persons rather than on impersonal systems of official bureaucracy when in need of assistance.[22] The padrino (patron), someone of higher socio-economic status who may be relied upon for assistance and protection, and to whom one is then heavily obligated is part of personalism of "who you know". It is not unlike the patron system in many village societies.

The belief in spiritualism is widespread. Rogler & Hollingshead suggest that while many middle and upper class Puerto Ricans are more reluctant to discuss spiritualism once the investigator establishes rapport, persons of all social positions acknowledge beliefs in spirits and describe incidents to illustrate their beliefs.

> Spiritualism is the most prevalent form of social organization outside the family. Spiritualism is the one institution to which people turn for help in their hours of need. They know it will have the answer to their plaintive question. The medium understands their subculture, she knows how to placate the problem by plausible interpretation of their troubles. She provides social support to an emotionally disturbed person.[23]

The main form of family organization is patriarchal and extended. While the Latin stereotype of earlier days is waning somewhat, the dominant form continues to include the father as the boss and decision maker, with the mother running the household and raising the children. Children are expected to respect their fathers and revere their mothers. Any insult to the mother is the extreme offense and may be answered by violence.[24]

Although urbanization, changing housing patterns, and an increase in the number of more isolated nuclear family units is taking place, the importance of the extended family to Puerto Ricans is not to be underestimated. [25] Very distant relatives are part of the family, and when Puerto Ricans are introduced to each other they may trace family histories until some distant parentesco relationship is discovered. A stranger becomes accepted de la familia if some parentescos or a perentesca with a close friend is identified.

> "Roles of family members - father, mother, grandparents, children, aunts, brothers, sisters, godparents, cousins and in-laws are clearly defined. All adults living in a home, or visiting, share permanently or temporarily in parental responsibility toward the children. Children are taught to obey and respect all adults. Some sociological studies indicate that obedience and respect of parents and other adults are valued above love in Puerto Rican culture."[26]

Lewis' study of a particular slum in San Juan reported a varient picture.

> The traditional concept of the closely knit Puerto Rican family must be modified in the light of our investigation. Although within rural areas, as well as within urban slums, there was often a strong feeling

of solidarity among closely related individuals who lived nearby, contact between urban slum dwellers and their rural kin was weak and sporadic. When visiting did occur, it was urban migrant who usually went to see his rural relatives, rather than vice versa. Over half the families, however, did not visit them even once a year. Loss of contact with relatives who had migrated to New York was even more marked.[27]

Sex roles are clearly defined within the culture.

"Latin American men and women have unequivocal conceptions of their roles and they play them out, if not in harmony, at least in counterpoint. The interpersonal dynamics of the existing social structure afford each sex a complementary sphere of influence that satisfies basic personal and social needs."

Latin American women do not seem to want to change their role. Although they complain about their suffering and about how unfair men are, they seem to enjoy their "sadness", and make little effort to change their status.[28]

Stevens reports that adult male harassment of wives, mistresses, and female household members often includes unexplained absences from the home, deliberate lateness for meals, demands for menial services, stinginess and severe restriction of women's activity outside the home. Girls are taught to cater to their brothers and fathers; boys to treat their sisters with affectionate condescension and to look out for them - particularly when they are outside of the home.

Women play the game by training the children to shame the father for his demanding, stingy, or unfaithful behavior, and to support and admire the mother for her suffering. This is likely to occur regardless of the woman's capacity as a mother and homemaker. Women are described as morally and spiritually superior to men. However, this superiority can only be demonstrated by women's suffering responses to male aggressive macho behavior. Thus, male harassment is necessary for the display of female superiority.[29]

Hidalgo describes the virginity cult among Puerto Ricans as one which demands total obedience to the husband. Since virginity is so highly prized, sexual experimentation by women is forbidden and women become fearful of experiencing and expressing sexual pleasure.

A married woman who is not promiscuous is considered to be a good wife, regardless of whatever other faults she may possess.

"Machismo is the quality that exemplifies man's superiority over women, the value of demonstrating by acts considered virile (such as fathering children, seducing women, being waited upon by women, avoiding tasks that are considered "women tasks", that the man is macho completo (all man). It allows man complete freedom in sexual expression as often with the knowledge and tacit consent of the wife."[30]

Steven remarks that a description of stereotypic machista behavior by some Latin American writers reads like a listing of the seven deadly sins. These behaviors include: pride or arrogance, an overbearing attitude, hypersensitivity, wrath, not only violence but stubbornness, and refusal to modify or retreat from a position, aggressiveness at all times, even if it leads to danger, disgrace, or ridicule. The only safe aggression is that directed against women as sexual conquests. Sexual hyperactivity is expected. Disdain and cruelty toward women are appropriate for a man, except toward his mother, who is treated as a saint. All of these behaviors require a male audience if the practitioner is to maintain his <u>machista</u> status.[31]

Culture Conflict

Fitzpatrick and Gould summarize the concepts of cultural strain, or value conflict which may contribute to emotional problems as follows: 1) contradictions in the values which govern male, in contrast to female behavior, may lead to anxieties in the man about machismo, in a female, to a martyr complex or excessive fear resulting from cloistering; 2) problems centering on the mother-son relationship may lead to frustration in the son, difficulty in overcoming dependency on women or in establishing an adequate love relationship with a wife; severe depression may develop in women who seek to respond to an idealized female role; 3) authority patterns are strong in Puerto Rico, and if they become excessive, they may generate hostility against authority figures; 4) the keen sense of personal dignity (<u>dignidad</u>); and the emphasis on respect (<u>respeto</u>) may build up a potential for violence; 5) the overwhelming burden of poverty and the accumulation of problems of the poor may make the difference between mental health and mental illness. A specific form of hysteria called "the Puerto Rican Syndrome" is mentioned by many authors. This is called the <u>ataque</u> by Puerto Ricans. It is a tendency to resort to a hyperkinetic seizure at a time of acute tensions and anxiety.[32]

Communication

Fundamental to the practice of social work is two-way communication. The social worker must both initiate and receive messages. Language is the primary device for communicating such messages, even though it is not the only one. Therefore, the knowledge of the client's language is essential.

Garcia refers to the fact that clients were made to feel guilty and inferior by the social worker because they knew no English. Of course, the social workers knew no Spanish. He describes situations, with which we are very familiar, where a small child had to serve as interpreter for the client, and when a neighbor had to serve as interpreter and respond to questions of a very personal nature which were not appropriate for the neighbor to hear.

> Language skills and facility are crucial to the understanding of any culture, especially if the student hopes to know the culture from within... But language learning is invaluable because there is an intimate and inevitable relationship between the language structure of a culture and the modes in which the people think and act, and because language is the ordinary and most distinctively human way in which people communicate their concepts and state their judgments.
>
> People of any culture can think only the thoughts their language permits them to think, and their language in turn helps them construct their universe.[33]

The importance of language is further illustrated in the field of linguistics:

> It was found that the background linguistic system (in other words, the grammar) of each language is not merely a reproducing instrument for voicing ideas but rather is itself the shaper of ideas, the program and guide for the individual's mental stock and trade.[34]

Barna cites five barriers to accurate communication across cultures:

1. Language differences
2. Non-Verbal communication.
3. Stereotypes that provide structure to raw experience and become realized through "self-fulfilling prophecy".
4. The tendency to evaluate content of communication in terms of the cultural orientation of the receiver of the communication.
5. The high level of anxiety which shrouds cross-cultural communication dealing with unfamiliar experiences.

Another element to be considered in cross-cultural training is non-verbal communication.[35] Channels of non-verbal communication to be understood include:

1. Kinesics - movement of the body (head, arms, leg, etc.)

2. Proxemics - use of interpersonal space.

3. Chronemics - the timing of verbal exchanges during conversation.

4. Oculesics - eye to eye contact or avoidance.

5. Haptics - the tactile form of communication.[36]

A Special Source of Cross-Cultural Training

The source of material useful to the social worker in dealing with a different cultural group can be the group itself. Camarillo and Del Buono[37] suggest that social work education could be vastly improved through the utilization of barrio experiences and the development of barrio perspective.

> Barrio persons without traditional academic credentials have a vast knowledge gained from intense life experience. Some barrio input to challenge monocular view of social problems reflecting individual rather than social deficits is vitally needed.
>
> Possibilities include utilizing barrio residents as professors, detaching departments, program field placements and instructors from the campus of a school and locating them in barrios. Barrio professors could work together with accredited social work professors on a team basis, each affecting and learning from the other. Although lecture, reading and classroom material can provide important cross-cultural learning, non-traditional inputs from the client group are of primary value.[38]

The complicated nature of the communication process across cultural lines and the variety of factors that enter into an understanding of another culture called for a unique type of training for the social work students who were the participants in this project. In both cognitive and experiential aspects, the program required unique approaches that extended beyond the normal education of social workers.

Footnotes:

1. Julius Gould & William L. Kolb (Eds.) A Dictionary of the Social Sciences. (New York: The Free Press, 1964), p. 165.

2. Robert A. Levine. Culture, Behavior and Personality. (Chicago: Aldine Publishing Company, 1973), p. 20.

3. Ralph Kolodony. "Ethnic Cleavages in the United States". Social Work, Vol. XIV (January, 1969).

4. Alejandro Garcia. "The Chicano and Social Work", in La Causa Chicana: The Movement for Justice, Margaret M. Mangold (Ed.) (New York: Family Service Association of America, 1972-73) p. 106.

5. Joseph Giordano. Ethnicity and Mental Health. National Project on Ethnic America of the American Jewish Committee. Institute of Human Relations, 165 East 56 Street, New York, New York, 1973, p. 11

6. Hugh Graham and Ted R. Gurr. The History of Violence in America. (New York: Bantam Books, 1969), p. XIV, as quoted in Ethnicity and Mental Health by Joseph Giordano, op. cit.

7. Garcia, op. cit. p. 109.

8. Readings in Intercultural Communication, Vol. 111, the Intercultural Communications Network of the Regional Council for International Education, (June, 1973) p. 7.

9. John E. Walsh. Intercultural Education in the Community of Man. (Honolulu: University Press of Hawaii, 1973), p. 8.

10. Daniel Sanders. "Educating Social Workers for the Role of Effective Change Agents in a Multi-Cultural, Pluralistic Society", Journal of Education for Social Work (Spring, 1974), Vol. 10, #2, p. 87.

11. Ibid, p. 92

12. John B. Turner, "Education for Practice with Minorities", Social Work, (May, 1972), Vol. 17, #3, p. 113.

13. John P. Gillin, "Modern Latin-American Culture", Portrait of Society, Eugenio Fernandez Mendez (ed.). San Juan, Puerto Rico: University of Puerto Rico Press, 1972, p. 12.

14. Ibid, p. 3

15. William Davidson, "Rural Latin American Culture". Portrait of a Society, Eugenio Fernandez Mendez (ed.) op. cit. p. 23

16. Ibid, p.

17. Florence R. Kluckhohn and Fred L. Strodtbeck. Variations in Value Orientations Elmsford, N. Y.: Row, Peterson, 1961, p. 12

18. The value orientations cited are heavily derived from Kluckhohn & Strodtbeck (cited earlier) and from Sidney W. Mintz. "Puerto Rico: An Essay on the

Definition of a National Culture". Status of Puerto Rico: Selected Background Studies for the United States-Puerto Rico Commission on the Status of Puerto Rico. Washington, D.C. U. S. Gov't. Printing Office, 1966.

19. For general discussion of traditions and values see such works as: Joseph P. Fitzpatrick Puerto Rican Americans, (Englewood Cliffs, N.J.: Prentice-Hall, 1971); Elena Padilla. Up From Puerto Rico (New York: Columbia University Press, 1958): Oscar Lewis. A Study of Slum Culture (New York: Random House): Fernandez-Mendez. Portrait of a Society (San Juan: University of Puerto Rico Press, 1972); F. Cordasco & E. Bucchioni. The Puerto Rican Experience (Totwa, N. J.: Adams, Littlefield, 1973); Sidney W. Mintz Worker in the Cane (New Haven: Yale University Press, 1960); S. Mintz "An Essay in the Definition of National Culture", in: Status of Puerto Rico. (Washington, D.C.: Government Printing Office, 1966); and C. W. Mills et al, The Puerto Rican Journey. (New York: Russell & Russell, 1967).

20. Hilda Hidalgo. "The Puerto Rican", Ethnic Differences Series (Washington, D.C.: National Rehabilitation Association, 1973) p. 57.

21. Hidalgo. The Puerto Rican, op. cit., pp. 57-58.

22. Fitzpatrick, op. cit., p. 89-92.

23. Lloyd H. Rogler & August B. Hollingshead. Trapped: Families and Schizophrenia: (New York: Wiley, 1965), p. 260.

24. Kal Wagenheim. Puerto Rico: A Profile. (New York: Praeger, 1970) p. 89.

25. C. W. Mills, et al. The Puerto Rican Journey. (New York: Russell & Russell, 1967) p. 8; Wagenheim, op. cit. p. 190; Fitzpatrick, op. cit. p. 89-92.

26. Hidalgo, op. cit., p. 62.

27. Oscar Lewis. A Study of a Slum Culture (New York: Random House, 1970) p. 106.

28. Evelyn P. Stevens. "Machismo and Marignismo", Society, Vol. 3, #6 (September/October, 1973), p. 57.

29. Ibid p. 63.

30. Hidalgo, op. cit., p. 63.

31. Stevens, op. cit., p. 58-61

32. Joseph Fitzpatrick & Robert E. Gould. "Mental Illness Among Puerto Ricans in New York: Cultural Conditions or Intercultural Misunderstanding?" Joint Commission on Mental Health for Children, Chevy Chase, Maryland. The following works are references noted by Fitzpatrick and Gould. H. B. Green. "Comparison of Nurturance and Independence Training in Jamaica and Puerto Rico, with Consideration of the Resulting Personality Structure and Transplanted Social Patterns", Journal of Social Psychiatry, 51:27-63, (1960): David Landy. Tropical Childhood: Cultural Transmission and Learning in a Rural Puerto Rican Village. Chapel Hill, University of North Carolina Press, 1959: E. P. Maldanado Sierra & R. D. Trent. "The Sibling Relationship in Group Psychotherapy with Puerto Rican Schizophrenics", American Journal of Psychiatry, 117:239-43, (1960): Oscar Lewis, La Vida: A Puerto Rican Family in the Culture of Poverty San Juan and New York. New York: Random House, 1966: R. Marina-Fernandez, "The Puerto Rican Syndrome: Its Dynamics and Cultural Determinants", Psychiatry, 24: 79-82, (1961)

33. Walsh, op. cit., p. 64.

34. Michael Cole, et. al. The Cultural Context of Learning and Thinking.
    (New York Basic Books, 1971), p. 10.

35. L. M. Barna. "Stumbling Blocks in Interpersonal Intercultural Communications",
    in: Readings in Intercultural Communications, David Hoopes (Ed.) (Pittsburg:
    University of Pittsburgh, 1970).

36. Melvin Schnapper. "Your Actions Speak Louder", The Volunteer, (June, 1969).
    Shirley Weitz. Non-Verbal Communication. New York, Oxford University Press,
    1974. Edward T. Hall. The Silent Language. Greenwich, Conn. Fawcett, 1959.
    The Hidden Dimension, Garden City, New York, Doubleday, 1966. Albert E. Schef-
    flin. Body Language and Social Order, Englewood Cliffs, New Jersey, Prentice
    Hall, 1972.

37. Maeteo Camrillo & Antonio Del Buono. "Utilizing Barrio Expertise in Social
    Work Education", in The Movement for Justice, Margaret Mangold (Ed.),
    op. cit.

38. Ibid.

CHAPTER 2

EDUCATIONAL RATIONALE

The educational frame of reference of the project staff derived from general concepts of learning from such sources as Hilgard[1] and Bruner[2] and, those more familiar efforts to relate learning theory to social work education of Tyler[3] and Knowles.[4] General systems theory[5], theories of human communication[6], and exploration of cultural variables in behavior[7], also influenced the project staff. A kind of theoretical amalgam plus a process of mutual education occurred which fits Bruner's description:

> Learning and problem solving are divisible into phases. These have been described by different writers. But all descriptions agree on one essential feature: that there is a cycle involving the formulation of a testing procedure or trial, the operation of this testing procedure and the comparison of the results of the test with some criterion. It has variously been called trial and error, means-end testing, trial and check, discrepancy reduction, test-operate-test-exit (TOTE), hypothesis testing, and so on... Knowledge of results should come at a point when the person is comparing the results of his try-out with some criterion of what he seeks to achieve.[8]

The project staff team utilized feedback from participating students, field, and class faculty to this end. The result was an educational "process" in part planned and in part serendipidous.

The analysis offered loosely parallels that presented by Somers[9] who addressed: the individual learner, the group situation, the social system (the teaching-learning transaction) and its relationship to the larger system, and the teacher. Our reordering starts with some assumptions about learning: the role of the teacher, the role of the student, the group process and the educational experience.

Somers suggests:

> ...it is the knowledge component which brings the learner and the teacher together, that invites and sustains their relationships, interactions and collaborative work...[10]

Without both student and teacher shared interest and concern for specific issues and problems, there is no basis for their communicating. Knowles' orientation to the learning of adults also values knowledge, but knowledge which is centered on solutions to current problems, rather than on subject matter developed in a logical sequence for future use.[11]

He defines adult learning (andragogy) "...not as a process of transmitting knowledge but as a process of inquiry" which he relates to the life cycle and the shift in self concept of the learner from dependence in childhood to increasing self direction and independence in adolescence and adulthood. This conceptualization suggests particular roles for both student and teacher in the learning process. These were the roles fostered by the project staff.

19

In the development of the project curriculum, the focus was a series of experiences which were consistent with what Knowles describes as specific experiences and action-learning techniques (including discussion, laboratory experiments, simulations, field experiences, collaborative team efforts, etc.) and the involvement of the learners in an analysis of the specific experience. Thus the focus of teaching becomes increasingly centered on inquiry rather than on the transmission of information. Learning concentrates on the nature of problems to be solved and tasks to be mastered, on the exploration of alternatives, and on the new problems and tasks discovered in these efforts at solution and mastery. It would thus appear that the formulation of a problem and a system of inquiry may be more important than the development of a specific solution. Man is viewed as a stimulus seeking, problem solving creature who seeks a degree of new tension in finding tasks to be mastered in his environment. This conception is considerably removed from the notion of an equilibrium model of behavior and from the stimulus response concept. The goal of behavior is not seen as tension reduction to meet the requirement of a steady state and the maintenance of equilibrium. The tendency for human personality to go beyond the steady state and to strive for enhancement and elaboration even at the cost of considerable disequilibrium has been elaborated in psychological literature.[12]

The closed system view of an exchange of material and energy in a stimulus response system in which the individual proceeds from needs gratification to tension reduction to equilibrium is abandoned. It is replaced by an open system view with spontaneous autonomous stimulus seeking exploratory behavior which makes for growth and change and self realization. This open system view rests heavily on the notion of the feedback phenomenon. "...by feedback is meant a communications network which produces action in response to an input of information and includes the results of its own action in the new information by which it modifies its subsequent behavior."[13] That is, a portion of the output effect or information about the output effect fed back to the input influences the subsequent behavior at the input. Feedback as a concept has been known in engineering technology for perhaps 150 years, has been used in electronics for at least 50 years and in various ways in educational theory for perhaps 30 years.[14]

The Teacher's Role

Bruner has referred to two kinds of teaching: the expository mode and the hypothetical mode.[15] In the expository mode, content is principally determined by the teacher as expositor and the teacher has a wide choice of alternatives and can manipulate the content. The student as listener and recipient has few options in this paternalistic model, and rewards are extrinsic in the form of grades. In the hypothetical mode the student is not viewed as a passive listener but has a part in the formulation of content and goals. This mode encourages exploration and discovery, and the rewards become intrinsic. The conscious stance adopted by the project staff to achieve optimal involvement of the learners, was that of facilitator, resource person, questioner, and not that of expert or fountainhead of all knowledge.[16]

The teaching team on the project viewed the facilitator-resource person role as the beginning point of contact with each student group. The end point, initially implied and later made explicit, was that in the process, teacher and student would join forces in joint exploration and investigation and that the discreet distinctions between teacher and learner would become increasingly vague in this sharing process.

It was the teaching team's responsibility to define the arena in which learning experiences would be shared and to make avilable some "tools" in the form of rudimentary bibliographies and a number of experiences in field and classroom. Students were encouraged to select other subsequent experiences which would be relevant for the group or for themselves as individuals.

The project staff team also took responsibility for creating the atmosphere in which learning could be facilitated by having frequent relatively informal group meetings and by attempting to "model" open, trustful, non-defensive behavior and inquiry.[17]

Cognitive and affective screens against which selected experiences could be examined by the teaching team and students together were designed by faculty as follows: The cognitive screen consisted of questions about practice, questions about research, and questions about social policy which might be raised from the specific experience recently encountered. The affective screen consisted of the identification of value premises, assumptions and attitudinal responses to the learning experience.

The cognitive and affective screens through which the experience could be filtered in a feedback session, following the experience, was to lead to conceptualizations, integration and a new base from which to begin the next learning experience. It was also assumed that this conceptualization and integration would lead to new practice behaviors. Since social work is a practice profession, the major concern remained with the consequences for practice of all the activities undertaken.

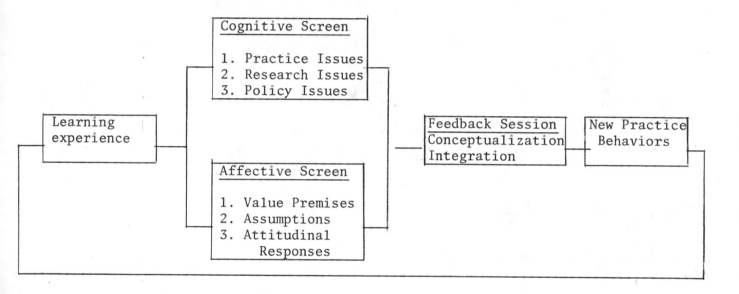

The Student's Role

> We have finally begun to absorb into our culture the ancient insight that the heart of education is learning, not teaching, and so our focus has started to shift from what the teacher does to what happens to the learner.[18]

Fifteen years ago, Tyler[19] exhorted teachers to shift their learning objectives from what the teachers wanted to teach to the learning behavior outcomes expected in the students (knowledge, attitude, skill).

Implicit in this project from its inception was the notion that students who were highly motivated, self-directed, and interested in exploring and developing other vehicles for social work education would be encouraged to participate. The project by its very nature stimulated the interest of students who were somewhat iconoclastic and not entirely satisfied with the existing system of education within the School of Social Work. It also required an interest in drug abuse and Puerto Rican migrants by its subject foci. A degree of student self awareness, security and a willingness to risk oneself in facing not only a different educational design which was evolving, but the specific experiences of living with a family in another culture, and learning a new language were of high priority. Students who applied for participation in this program were clearly a self-selected sample who came with a variety of motivations. Faculty criteria for acceptance included estimates of motivation, capacities, past experience with other cultures or sub-cultures (in many instances students had experiences abroad with Peace Corps or other organizations, a substantial number had traveled to foreign countries, and some had extensive experience with minority groups and particular sub-cultures in this country).

It has been suggested that social work students are sometimes viewed as clients, products, subjects, observers, interacters, scholars, trainees, and emerging personalities.[20] Project staff and students both had only a rather loose general model of the competency required at the end of the training year. Faculty team tended to define the students as part trainee, part scholar and part peer learner, with some assumptions about the "maturing experience" of facing oneself in an alien culture. It was also assumed that students would learn some things deductively, but that more of the learning would take place in a pragmatic eclectic effort to examine the nature of problems, alternatives and solutions.

Footnotes:

1. Ernest Hilgard and G. H. Bowers. _Theories of Learning,_ 3rd edition, (New York: Appleton-Century-Crofts, 1966).

2. Jerome S. Bruner. _Toward a Theory of Instruction._ (Cambridge, Mass.: Harvard University Press, 1966). p. 19

3. Ralph Tyler, et. al. "Analysis of the Purpose, Pattern, Scope and Structure of the Officer Education Program of Air University", Officer Education Research Laboratory, Air Force Personnel and Training Research Center, Air Research and Development Command, Maxwell Air Force Base, Alabama, May, 1955.

4. Malcolm S. Knowles. "Innovations in Teaching Styles and Approaches Based on Adult Learning". _Journal of Education for Social Work,_ Vol. 8, #2, (Spring, 1972).

5. General Systems Theory: See C. West Churchman. _The Systems Approach._ (New York: Delta, 1968).

6. Communications Theory: See P. Watzlawich, J. Bevan, and D. D. Jackson. _Pragmatics of Human Communications._ (New York: Norton, 1967).

7. Cultural Concepts and Behavior: See Jane Murphy and Alexander H. Leighton. _Approaches to Cross Cultural Psychiatry._ (Ithaca: Cornell University Press, 1965); Marvin K. Opler. _Culture and Social Psychiatry._ (New York: Atherton, 1967); and D. R. Price-Williams. _Cross Cultural Studies._ (Baltimore: Penguin, 1969).

8. Jerome Bruner, _op. cit._ pg. 50-51

9. Mary L. Somers, "Dimensions and Dynamics of Engaging the Learner." _Journal of Social Work Education,_ Vol. 7, #3 (Fall, 1971).

10. _Ibid._ p. 50

11. Knowles, _op. cit._

12. G. W. Allport. "The Open System in Personality Theory", in: _Modern Systems Research for the Behavioral Scientist,_ Walter Buckley (Ed.) (Chicago, Aldine, 1968).

13. Carl W. Deutsch. "Towards a Cybernetic Model of a Man in Society". in: _Modern Systems Research for Behavioral Scientist,_ op. cit., pp. 390-91. See also: Ludwig Von Bertalanfsky. "General Systems Theory" A Critical Review". in _Modern Systems Research for Behavioral Scientist,_ op. cit.

14. Hilgard & Bower, _op. cit._; Tyler, _op. cit._

15. Bruner, _op. cit._

16. Beulah Rothman. "Perspectives on Learning and Teaching in Continuing Education", _Journal of Education for Social Work,_ Vol. 9, #2 (Spring, 1973). Also see, Knowles, _op. cit._

17. O. H. Mowrer. "The Behavior Therapies, with Special Reference to Modeling and Imitation". _American Journal of Psychotherapy,_ Vol, 20, (1966), pp. 439-461.

18.   Knowles, _op. cit._, p. 33.

19.   Tyler, _op. cit._

20.   Charles Guzzetta.   "Curriculum Alternatives", Journal of Education for Social Work, Vol. 8, #7 (Winter, 1972).

CHAPTER 3

SELECTED CENSUS DATA ABOUT PUERTO RICAN POPULATION
ON MAINLAND U. S. A.

1. Rules Governing Data Selection

In order to provide the reader with some factual data against which he may check his, or an imaginary average New Yorker's perception of Puerto Ricans, selected data from the U. S. Census of 1970[1] are presented. Data covering mainly New York City are given. One reason is that New York City has the greatest concentration of Puerto Ricans on the mainland. Another is that the Hunter College School of Social Work is located in and involved with the City, and so, therefore, was the Project. It is the people who come to the attention of the City's health, education and welfare agencies who will mainly be served by the graduates of the Project. It appears that the New York City data are fairly typical for the whole metropolitan area.

The variables selected for description and a brief analysis are: population, educational level, income, occupation and welfare involvement.

Our main interest was to determine whether second and third generation Puerto Ricans born on the mainland (defined by the Census as persons "of Puerto Rican parentage" and abbreviated by us as "P") are different from Island-born first generation Puerto Ricans (defined by the Census as "of Puerto Rican birth, and abbreviated by us as "B").

2. Population by Sex and Age[2]

Male	TOTAL B OR P					
	N	%	N	%	N	%
All males	388,080	100	215,142	55.4	172,938	44.6
Males under 24	230,674	100	72,341	31.4	158,333	68.6
Female						
All females	429,632	100	258,158	60.1	171,474	39.9
Females under 24	247,705	100	82,351	33.2	165,354	66.8
Total						
All male and female	817-712	100	473,300	57.9	344,412	42.1
Male and female under 24	478,379	100	154,692	32.3	323,687	67.7

The table indicates that, while the majority of New York Puerto Ricans are of Puerto Rican birth, a good two-thirds of those under 24 were born on the mainland. There has been a consistent increase in the Puerto Rican parentage group ever since 1950.[3] This indicates that the city now clearly has a self-propagating community - a fact which must be taken into consideration in policy-making. And although we as well as many others talk about the commuter migration, we may not forget that this community appears to be more and more New York - or mainland - born.

3. Educational Level[4]

Years of school completed Age 25 and over	B	P
Median	8.4	11.2
% High school graduates	18.0	42.0

This table gives a strong picture of upward educational mobility. It is complemented by yet another statistic:[5]

Years of school completed Males 25 to 34 years old	B		P	
	N	%	N	%
Total ever to school	53,816	100	7,580	100
High school up to 3 years	18,864	35.1	2,148	28.3
College Completed	558	1.0	235	3.1
Females 25 to 34 years old				
Total ever to school	64,459	100	8,534	100
High school up to 3 years	19,328	30	2,621	30.7
College completed	572	0.9	140	1.6

This table indicates that in the group of younger adults, most of whom are not likely to go on in their schooling, we have an overwhelming majority with only elementary schooling or some high school. To the extent that education is an entrance ticket to higher-level jobs, it would seem that such jobs will remain unavailable to a great many Puerto Ricans.

Note that there are few college graduates. However, the census lists a considerably larger number of men and women with up to 3 years of college. Since at least the younger part of this 25 to 34 group may well pursue their college education and complete it, there seems to be yet another indication of an upward educational push.

4. Income

Lower educational level leads to lower-level jobs and, of course, lower income.[6]

Median Income	B	P
All families	N=184,339	N=18,610
Median income	$5,514	$6,381
Mean income	$6,208	$7,031

Income less than poverty level

Number of families	56,741	4,696
% of "All families" above	30.3	25.2
Number of families with female head	31,404=17% of "all"	2,757=14.8% of "all"
Mean size of family	4.48	3.91
Mean income deficit	$1,771	$1,703

Here we begin to get the picture of the mainland-born Puerto Ricans being better off than the Puerto Rico-born. They have better education and somewhat better income. Perhaps they could also be described as being better acculturated to North American ways in that they have fewer families with female heads (though the percentage difference is small), and fewer children.[7]

5. Occupation

The occupational groups to which Puerto Ricans belong are recorded in the U. S. Census of 1970. Fitzpatrick[8] examined the 1950 and 1960 census data and stressed the "impressive progress" made by the second-generation Puerto Ricans. Briefly, his interpretation is that men and women tended to move upward in their jobs with some of the strongest movement being from the blue-collar operatives group to the white-collar clerical group.[9]

For 1970, the data are as follows:[10]

Major occupational groups

	B		P	
	N	%	N	%
Males employed, 16 and over	127,645	100	19,831	100
Professional, technical and kindred workers	4,041	3.2	1,431	7.2
Managers and adm., exc. farm	5,562	4.4	981	4.9
Sales workers	5,969	4.7	1,421	7.2
Clerical and kindred workers	16,095	12.6	4,471	22.5
Craftsmen, foremen and kindred	19,666	15.4	3,052	15.4
Operatives, incl. transport	40,426	31.7	3,966	20.0
Laborers, exc. farm	7,165	5.6	1,529	7.7
Farmers and farm managers	34	-	-	-
Farm laborers and foremen	146	.1	43	.2
Service workers, exc. private households	28,379	22.2	2,912	14.7
Private household workers	161	.1	25	.1
Females employed, 16 and over	55,611	100	13,371	100
Prof., techn. and kindred	3,163	5.7	1,170	8.7
Managers and adm., exc. farm	905	1.6	241	1.8
Sales workers	2,133	3.8	822	6.1
Clerical and kindred	15,747	28.3	7,989	59.7
Craftsmen, foremen and kindred	1,612	2.9	142	1.1
Operatives, incl. transport	24,455	44.0	1,466	11.0

Major occupational groups (Continued)

	B		P	
	N	%	N	%
Laborers, exc. farm	633	1.1	44	.3
Farmers and farm managers	-	-	24	.2
Farm laborers and foremen	12	-	-	-
Service workers exc. private households	6,497	11.7	1,395	10.4
Private household workers	454	.8	78	.6

If we look at these data in terms of whether the mainland-born males hold better jobs than the Puerto Rico-born, we find that indeed they do; the heaviest job concentration for males is in clerical work, and they are consistently higher in white collar employment generally. A similar pattern holds for the women, with an even higher concentration in clerical work.

We cannot directly compare our data with those of Fitzpatrick as he arranged the census groups somewhat. By and large, we can identify some mobility from the "operative" to the "clerical and sales" group, but there is little question that progress has been rather modest.

6. Welfare

We noted above (under income) that 30.3% of New York City's Puerto Rican families earn an income below poverty level, and suffer a mean income deficit of $1,766 (the average of both B and P; on p. 30 above B and P are listed separately).

The census data offer some information on how this deficit is made up in New York State (New York City data are not given but there seems to be a general presumption that most welfare is "handed out" in the city, and there must be some truth to this since the vast majority of Puerto Ricans live in the metropolitan area).

Type of income of families	B		P	
	N	%	N	%
All families	194,610	100	20,696	100
With wage or salary income	142,741	73.3	15,999	76.3
Mean wage or salary income	$7,058		$8,368	
With public assistance or public welfare income	57,440	29.5	4,682	22.6
Mean PA or PW income	$2,447		$2,349	

We can draw two conclusions from these data. The first is that three quarters of the Puerto Rican families included in the census earn all or some of their living, though their earnings are at a low level.

The other conclusion is, of course, that dependence on public assistance and public welfare monies is fairly extensive, and somewhat heavier on the part of Puerto Rico-born families than on mainland-born families.

A one-sentence summary: mainland-born Puerto Ricans are generally better off than those who came to the city from Puerto Rico - but they certainly are not well off.

Footnotes:

1. The source for all data in this chapter is: U. S. Bureau of the Census. 1970 Census of Population. Subject Reports: Puerto Ricans in the United States. PC(2)-1E, June, 1973.

2. Ibid., Table 17, p. 107.

3. Ibid., Table 1, p. XL.

4. Ibid., Table 13, p. 102.

5. Ibid., Table 17, p. 107.

6. Ibid., Table 25, p. 117.

7. This presentation is descriptive, and we are only noting some of the more salient differences. No attempt at evaluating the statistical significance of differences is made.

8. Fitzpatrick,J. G. Puerto Rican Americans: The Meaning of Migration to the Mainland. (Englewood Cliffs, N.J.: Prentice-Hall, 1971), p. 60ff.

9. Occupations as grouped by the census do not form a rank order or hierarchy in terms of social or skill levels (U.S. Census, 1970; PC(2)1-E, App, C, p. 11). Of course the common social perception implies precisely such a hierarchy, which is reflected in terms of income and social status.

10. U.S. Census, op cit., Table 25, p. 117.

11. Ibid., Table 9, p. 93.

CHAPTER 4

THE NEW YORK PUERTO RICAN COMMUNITY

Everyday Observations

If the New Yorker is a middle class person, he will have the superficial contact one has with taxi drivers, waiters, doormen and elevator operators. The contact will usually be friendly enough and made easy by the fact that the participants in such encounters simply perform their prescribed roles and then go about their own business.

If the New Yorker rides the buses or subways, he will see a great many Puerto Ricans, mostly as passengers. Few of them are bus drivers, conductors, or Transit Authority patrolmen. These positions of authority are occupied by whites and (more and more) black North Americans. What he will often see is a bewildered stranger trying to get to the Bronx, or to find the subway passage that will lead him from the "downtown" to the "uptown" side. The stranger may hold out a piece of paper with a Queens address, and the New Yorker may be unable to help because all he knows of Queens is that it is a place with a peculiar street-numbering system which causes everyone to get lost. If the New Yorker tries his halting Spanish on the stranger, he may well be shamed by a response which reveals a distinctly superior command of the English language.

The New Yorker may live close enough to a Hispanic section to experience some of the pertinacious efforts to settle down and make one's place in the way that successive waves of immigrants have done. He will see more and more Spanish restaurants. He will see the neighborhood bodega owner purchasing the tenement in which his basement grocery is located. And he will see that building filling up with ever more Hispanics who may be relatives or people from the new owner's hometown. The new owner will at first find, odd jobs for his tenants, and slowly help them to become part of the existing world of work.

Slowly, the newcomers work their way up. In the building maintenance trades, the men placed as cleaning men and general helpers may graduate to the post of superintendent. In the restaurant business, the men who start as dishwashers may become busboys and eventually waiters.

In that old-time New York institution, the Jewish delicatessen, the helper is likely to be Hispanic. The tradition of day-and-night work by a husband-and-wife team is disappearing as the owner becomes an absentee owner or supervisor, and (especially if the neighborhood gets to be "Portorican") sells out to the newcomer.

To the New Yorker, all Latins look the same and speak the same incomprehensible language. Therefore he does not know that a good deal of this social mobility is actually controlled by relatively well-to-do people from other Latin islands and countries, especially Cubans. Nor does he know that his development creates quite a bit of tension among the various Hispanic groups.

The Media

What the New Yorker learns about the work and social roles of Puerto Ricans is necessarily distorted by the peculiar perspectives of even respectable newspapers and television networks, for which only bad news is news. He is sure to learn about fires in tenements, floods in slum areas, and greedy landlords - all of which create more needy Puerto Rican "cases" out in the street. He is sure to hear about crimes of passion (that Latin temperament!), robberies and other kinds of assaultive and socially disapproved behavior, not to mention the terror of drug addiction. If he is not already afraid of these strangers, he is sure to be made so by the media which reinforce the common mechanisms of ethnic and linguistic prejudice.

I   It is important to note that this reinforcement of prejudice is largely unintentional. The presentation in a newscast is at least "objective" and often (especially in the case of fires, floods and eviction) sympathetic to the victim. But the impression made on the viewer or reader is that Puerto Ricans are offenders or victims, that they disturb the social order; it does not take a big leap to jump to the conclusion that the City would be ever so much better off if the whole lot of them went back to where they came from.

Not a few efforts have been made to counteract this negative stereotype. The television networks have learned (under political pressure) that they must have at least one Puerto Rican in a visible position. There he or she will usually report the human interest stories with which newscasts are rounded out just before the weather report. At least one such token Puerto Rican has handled this minor position in such a way that he has forced the New Yorker to face some hard facts about minority group slums, the treatment of the retarded in institutions, and so on. He may have done some good, and he certainly has followed in the tradition of the muckrakers of old. But by doing so, he is confirming the stereotype of Puerto Ricans as people with problems, or people who create problems.

Two television channels (both on ultra-high frequency and therefore difficult to tune in) are broadcasting in Spanish. Along with the usual mix of soap operas and other trivia, they present newscasts informing the viewer of happenings in Puerto Rico and other Latin areas, panel discussions on a wide variety of subjects, and often high-level cultural programs.

The New Yorker who accidentally hits one of these channels may only see that the commercials are often cheaply produced stills of the type last seen in movie houses decades ago. And he may register a mid-shock of estrangement when, as happens frequently, a Spanish-dubbed Hollywood movie is shown with say, John Wayne stepping out of the sheriff's office and greeting a fellow cowboy with a hearty shout of "Ola!", instead of the expected "Howdy".

The Spanish-language press has suffered the same shrinkage as have other newspapers. The remaining major daily is El Diario. One of the staff members who lives in an area heavily populated by Puerto Ricans and other Latins, checked out about 20 newsstands and other paper outlets in the neighborhood. Less than half carried the Diario. When the operators were asked why not, the most common response was that there was no demand for it. The operators of small stores carrying newspapers as a sideline would respond in a manner which was interpreted by the observer as an expression of suspicion, resentment, anger or defensiveness; overall, the tone of the response seemed to indicate that the operator did not want too many Puerto Ricans underfoot.

The average New Yorker, of course, would no more think of reading El Diario than he would any of the other papers published for a minority group other than his own.

El Desfile

        One way for minority groups to achieve visibility and demonstrate power
in New York is to have a parade, preferably one which is an institutionalized,
police-protected show that will catch the attention of the public and the media.
The Irish on St. Patrick's Day, the Italians on Columbus Day, the Jews on Israel
Independence Day, the Germans, the Poles, the Blacks and the homosexuals all have
their day in the sun.

        The Puerto Ricans have their annual parade as well, in late May or early
June. El Desfile is a major social event in the Puerto Rican community. It is
preceded by the election and coronation of the reina del desfile (the queen of the
parade), patterned on the Miss America contest. The coronation ceremony is invariably described as una emocionante celebración by the Hispanic media. Just as invariably, it is ignored by the English-language media. Politicians from the city and the
island always attend the parade, as one might expect. Quite a few mayors of the old
island hometowns fly up to march with their exiled townsmen. The hometown clubs try
to outdo each other in the number of marchers, the size and imaginativeness of the
floats, and the festiveness of the martial or dance tunes their bands are playing.
Both mainland and island television stations give full coverage to the event, with
countless on-the-spot interviews of Puerto Rican celebrities. The English-language
networks, however, will give the parade, at best, a minute or two on the regular
newscast, and emphasize the "local color" aspect. Press coverage is a little more extensive, especially when the politicians present are of some note.

        The New Yorker, who sees and hears more politicians than he cares to,
will give such reports barely a glance. He is use to ignoring minority group parades
(other than that of his own), and when he stumbles into one of them, he is likely
to perceive it mostly as an obstruction of traffic. El Desfile is no exception:
it is watched mostly by Puerto Ricans.

CHAPTER 5

PUERTO RICAN LITERATURE

In trying to orient ourselves in or about a country, it comes naturally to most of us to look for books about it. The historical and political literature about Puerto Rico is surprisingly rich, and certainly bewildering to the Anglo new-comer.

Historical and Political Literature about Puerto Rico

Among books written by North Americans, in English, a good survey account of Puerto Rico's history is given by Wagenheim[1] in which the historical narrative is importantly supplemented by an attempt to have Puerto Ricans of times past and present state views which are at variance with the official history. The fact that Puerto Ricans should also disagree among themselves, especially as regards the political and economic future of the island and its relationship to the United States, should come as no surprise to even a casual reader of newspapers. The fact that at least some Puerto Ricans take such disagreements very seriously, and indeed consider it quite literally a matter of life and death, may be a little more difficult to understand for the North American who is not in the habit of taking seriously the idea of Puerto Rico as a nation in the first place.

Another general survey in English deals primarily with that complementary aspect of recent Puerto Rican history, culture and politics without which no understanding of Puerto Rico can be achieved; the migration to the mainland.[2] The wealth of statistical data presented is unmatched by any other Anglo or Hispanic publication we know of.

At the time of this writing, these two volumes undoubtedly offer the most comprehensive English-language introduction to Puerto Rico on the Island and on the mainland.

If the New York or North American book-learner wishes to become acquainted with Puerto Rican perspectives as seen by Puerto Ricans, he is likely to go to one of the Spanish-language bookstores, of which there are quite a few in New York City. On 14th Street, a focal point of Hispanic cultural life, there are four within less than one block. Once more, one of the first things one learns is the apparent irrelevance of Puerto Rico as a historical, political or economic entity. The stores offer a rich selection of books by Spanish and Latin American authors. Of course, this reflects the fact that Spanish is one of the world's most widely spoken languages and that the numerous political entities, cultures and literatures which have come out of the former Spanish Empire form a whole world of their own. Puerto Rico is only a small province of this world, and an odd one at that because of its association with the United States.

A Puerto Rican poet, Luis Llorens Torres,[3] complained that it is a patito feo (an ugly duckling) which was never permitted to become a swan like its sister Latin American republics.

Puerto Rico is certainly one of the smaller of the Latin American nations, and one way of finding this out is to go to the largest Spanish-language bookstore, displaying hundreds of running feet of books from Spain, Mexico or the Argentine, or books about Cuba - and to find that Puerto Rico is relegated to a small niche in the back of the store.

The North American trying to learn Puerto Rican history as it is taught on the island might find a high school text such as Vivas' Historia de Puerto Rico[4]. The author laments the absence of an "official" history[5] and presents his textbook to fill the gap until such a history may be written. In its approach, then, it might be described as offering an "establishment" perspective largely supportive of the status quo - the Estado Libre Associado (Commonwealth). Therefore, the North American reader may be all the more jarred to find that the last section of the book, which deals with the period of United States sovereignty, is entitled El Trauma (The Trauma). This may be the first time he encounters that term. But as he progresses in his reading, he will find out that it is the accepted description for the American take-over of Puerto Rico in 1898. A more polite term is el cambio de soberanía (the change of sovereignty). The phrase, el trauma, gives fair warning to the naive reader of what the Puerto Rican experience of the island's involuntary association with the mainland has been - an experience in which disappointed hopes, confused expectations, and rage at a sovereign at best condescendingly negligent and at worst arrogantly oppressive are all inextricably mixed.

If an "establishment" text can be that critical, one will not be surprised that "anti-establishment" texts are even more so. Two of these texts, both of them histories and socio-political analyses of a more or less Marxist persuasion, have gained recognition even in circles clearly out of sympathy with the authors' political orientation.[6]

Puerto Rican Literature: Fiction, Poetry and Drama

A second book-learning avenue of orientation to Puerto Ricans is via their literary expression in fiction, poetry and drama. The easiest way of approaching this area is by getting acquainted with works written in English.

The work best known to the North American is undoubtedly Piri Thomas' Down These Mean Streets.[7] It is the autobiography of a new York-raised, dark-skinned Puerto Rican. Its themes are alienation in New York, racism both within the Puerto Rican culture and among the Anglos, pressure of peer groups toward drug use and separation from a family trying to preserve old values. These themes will soon become familiar to anyone trying to know more about Puerto Rico. Thomas' book has been a bestseller and has become a standard text for the many black and Puerto Rican studies programs which have sprouted in the groves of academe. His very success has won him some critical comments from Puerto Ricans. For example, here is a young poet talking:

> ...piri thomas selling his tissue paper red book and
>   singing dollar bills so loud...
> ...piri swinging high to my mama's clothing line film-
> ing and breeding
>   super-spic in disneyland
> and
>   not knowing that his days out of harlem
> have created
>   manteca[8] in his mind...[9]

Figueroa - a poet writing in English - also gives one a feeling of what it means to come up from the island as a child and to be exposed to the New York City public school system:

"SPANISH IS BAD FOR ME
 I WILL NOT SPEAK IT AGAIN"

>   /wen i didnt under stan an inglish wer/d
>   i wez dick tated to look-it up in
>   dear o'l webster's dichinery
>   an foun/dead he ate d SPA nish lan gwedge.10

The struggle of the immigrant with the language of the new country is not a novel theme in American literature. In fact, Figueroa's outrageous transcription of his dialect is oddly reminiscent of earlier attempts to convey linguistic estrangement. One example might be the Brooklyn Jewish in which much of the dialogue in Roth's Call it Sleep11 is rendered. In that novel, the children's street language is contrasted with the language of the parents (rendered in standard English but meant to be a translation of their Yiddish mother tongue, in which the highly prized old-country values and standards are conveyed).

It is no doubt an indication of the dual cultural-political identity as well as of the threat of accelerated (though resisted) assimilation that the kid who "didn't under stan an inglish wer/d" has become not only a university lecturer, but also an executive in the most important Puerto Rican educational agency of New York City.

The cultural and linguistic dual allegiance becomes more and more evident as one gets absorbed in Puerto Rican literature. The co-editor of a bilingual anthology of poetry12 offers a poem of his own:

>   del bronx el barrio la periferia convergen en manhattan
>   down town la fábrica
>   midtown porteros ascensoristas lavaplatos
>   cocineros salen del subway otro túnel
>   a/desde la muerte...13

He also presents his own English translation:

>   From the bronx spanish harlem the periphery converge in
>   manhattan
>   factories downtown
>   midtown porters elevator operators dishwashers
>   cooks come out of subways another tunnel
>   to/from death...14

But other young poets in this anthology are already writing in English, and the Spanish version of their work is done by a fellow Puerto Rican. Two examples:

>   Spics going to the cooker
>   never realizing they've
>   been cooked
>   Mind shook, money took
>   And nothing to show for it
>   but raw scars, railroad tracks
>   on swollen arms
>   And abscesses of the mind...15

```
...kingsize smoke/out of space/brooklyn bums
pickpocket thru the crowd/big fire of bright
ness brings day/darkness/darkness/the iron
horse/kicking in loudly/outside/dark/dark/life
the ladies of the boogaloo going by in hands/or
out of hands/in slow steps going by to cabs or
subways/the corners full with wide/eyed zombies
of the strange parts trying to buy a night for
themselves...16
```

If the reader has remained interested and adventurous enough to turn to the Puerto Rican literature written in the country's own language, he might first consult F. M. Cabrera's history of Puerto Rican literature. Cabrera, who teaches at the University of Puerto Rico, specifically states as one of his goals that he wishes to:

> place before the North American students and the U. S. people some pages which will help them to come to know and understand better some almost unknown aspect of our Puerto Rico.17

By now the North American student may no longer be taken aback by the description of the post-1898 period as that of el trauma.18

As the reader moves on to contemporary literature, he will find that the names of two authors with whom he may have become acquainted superficially through a variety of Anglo mentors are mentioned prominently: René Marqués and Pedro Juan Soto.

Marqués is best known for his play, La Carreta.19 It is the story of the decline and fall of a family moving from the hills of Puerto Rico to the slums of, first San Juan, and then New York.

Soto's early work20 is once more about the New York experience of strangers despised, ridiculed and abused by those who had come to the city before them.

In both of these works, the North American student, even if he has a reasonably good reading knowledge of Spanish, will run into a difficulty similar to that which he experiences when listening to Puerto Rican speech; much of the dialogue is rendered in the Puerto Rican dialectal pronunciation and idiomatic phrasing, as well as in "Spanglish". This can be a formidable obstacle to understanding, as our own students were to find out very soon.

It may seem as though we had been overly selective in this admittedly brief and incomplete survey, emphasizing materials concerning mainland relationships and the New York experience. This is not quite so. True, a good deal of Puerto Rican literature does not deal with el trauma or with New York. However, as we move from 1898 to the present day, those Puerto Rican writers who address themselves to social problems (and most of them do, even those whose themes are ostensibly private, non-political or folkloristic) have had to deal with the overriding fact that Puerto Rico as a society is intimately bound up with North American society - with ties that are political, economic, familial, cultural and linguistic. New York City, for better or for worse, is a second home to the Puerto Rican writer. English, for better or for worse, is his second language, and sometimes his first. He may dream of a return to traditional values as does the mother in Marqués' La Carreta.21 He may dream of hitching Puerto Rico's carreta to the star of anti-imperialist third-world revolution, as do so many in Matilla and Silén's Puerto Rican Poets. But if he is to speak about the real everyday world he and his protagonists live in, he has to come to terms with its unique bi-culturalism.

For Puerto Rican writers, therefore, the theme of allegiance to two cultures, two languages, and two countries joins the major themes of alienation, family dis-organization and dislocation and value conflicts between generations. And the background against which all of these themes are played is frequently poverty and slum life. In large measure, Puerto Rican literature is slum literature, a literature of poverty.

Footnotes:

1. Kal Wagenheim. <u>Puerto Rico: A Profile</u>. New York: Praeger, 1970.

2. Joseph P. Fitzpatrick, <u>op</u>. <u>cit</u>.,

3. Luis Llorens Torres. "El Patito Feo", in: Alfredo Matillo and Juan A. Silén, <u>Puerto Rican Poets/Los Poetas Puertarriqueños</u>. (New York: Bantam Books, 1972). p. 2. Pato and patito have a variety of pejorative meanings in colloquial Puerto Rican Spanish.

4. José Luis Vivas, Historia de Puerto Rico. New York: Las Americas, 1960.

5. <u>Ibid</u>., p. 7.

6. Oscar Lewis. <u>Freedom and Power in the Caribbean</u>. (New York: Monthly Review Press, 1964). Manuel Maldonado-Denis, <u>Puerto Rico: A Socio-Historic Interpretation</u>. (New York: Vintage Books, 1972).

7. Piri Thomas. <u>Down These Mean Streets</u>. (New York: Knopf, 1967).

8. <u>Manteca</u>: fat, lard, butter. In short, the author is calling Piri Thomas a fathead.

9. J. A. Figueroa. "East 110th Street", <u>East 110th Street</u>. Detroit, Michigan: Broadside Press, 1973, p. 25.

10. Figueroa, "111 Literate Poem", <u>op</u>. <u>cit</u>., p. 23.

11. H. Roth. <u>Call it Sleep</u> (1934). Reprint: New York: Avon Books, 1964.

12. Matilla and Silén, <u>op</u>. <u>cit</u>.

13. <u>Ibid</u>., "Subway", p. 116

14. <u>Ibid</u>., p. 117

15. <u>Ibid</u>., Luciano, "Message to a dope fiend", p. 202.

16. Hernandez Cruz, "Cocaine Galore 1", in: Matilla and Silén, <u>op</u>. <u>cit</u>., p. 210.

17. F. M. Cabrera. <u>Historia de la Literature Puertorriqueña</u>. (Rio Piedras, P.R.: Editorial Cultural, 1969), p. 11.

18. <u>Ibid</u>., p. 156

19. René Marqués. <u>La Carreta</u> (The Ox Cart) (1951). (Rio Piedras, P.R.: Editorial Cultural, 1963).

20. Pedro Juan Soto. <u>Spiks</u>. (1956) (Rio Piedras, P.R.: Editorial Cultural, 1970), 3rd edition.

21. Marqués, <u>op</u>. <u>cit</u>.

CHAPTER 6

IMMIGRATION AND ASSIMILATION

> The Jewish quarter of New York is generally supposed
> to be a place of poverty, dirt, ignorance and immor-
> ality - the seat of the sweatshop, the tenement house,
> where "red lights" sparkle at night, where the people
> are queer and repulsive. Well-to-do persons visit the
> ghetto merely from motives of curiosity of philanthropy;
> writers treat it sociologically, as a place in crying
> need of improvement.[1]

Doña Gabriela: No quiero que lo entieron en
                            ehta tierra sin sol.
                            Cohtara mucho llevarlo a
                            Puerto Rico?

Juanita: No importa lo que cuehte.[2]

The two epigraphs above are half a century apart in time. They are also far apart in spirit. Hapgood is an _Anglo_ outsider describing a population of new arrivals with sympathy and the best of intentions to correct popular stereotypes. Marqués, himself a sometimes resident of New York, describes the self-perception of a people who have a country to which they can return, albeit for burial.

Puerto Ricans are American citizens, and thus technically part of a domestic migration process. The dream of returning to _la isla_ and its reassuringly familiar social order can be realized with comparative ease. It is similar in many ways to the dream of the Southern Black migrant to the north who longs for _down home_ food, customs, warmth and civility, but is vastly different from the experience of the previous immigrants whose break with the _old country_ was far more radical.

However, both the average New Yorker and the social scientist persist in talking about Puerto Rican immigration. The Puerto Rican is perceived as an immigrant, someone very different from the fellow who moved from Ohio to New York because he found a better job here. The very number of Puerto Rican immigrants and their social status as a group encourage this kind of thinking. They are perceived by the _Anglo_ within the cognitive framework he has about immigrants.

What are the major features of this cognitive framework? The simplest way of approaching this is to examine some of the recurrent themes developed by those who have written the histories of our immigration history.

The mass movement of over 40 million people into a new land over a period of less than 200 years is awe-inspiring. The conventional wisdom was that America should be a melting pot. Old country customs, values and languages were to be abandoned; the newcomers were to become part of something vaguely described as the American mainstream, and to acquire something vaguely called the American national character. One thing reasonably clear to the old stock inhabitants was that it was better than anyone else's national character. Many social policies were developed to ensure that "melting" would take place. Immigration officers on Ellis Island might arbitrarily anglicize "unpronounceable" names. Efforts of linguistic groups (e.g., Germans in the Midwest, Spanish in New Mexico) to give their tongue some official status were resisted with special energy.

In time, conventional wisdom was translated into a popular sociological theory that it took three generations to make an American.[3]

All this melting was not without painful stresses. To begin with, there was the social Darwinism of the old stock residents. Few of those New Yorkers who hear the current hue and cry about the Negroes' alleged lack of intelligence or the Puerto Ricans' alleged instability and the threat these phenomena pose to the future of the nation remember that precisely the same accusations were leveled against earlier groups of immigrants. The popular view expressed by Hapgood (in the epigraph above) found its "scientific" expression through the voices of sociologists:

> The influx of a large immigrant population from peasant countries
> of central and southern Europe...gave color to the notion that
> immigration was lowering the standard of American intelligence...[4]

Popular and "scientific" views were translated into social programs by members of the medical profession and by social workers, and contributed to a major social policy shift: the restriction of immigration by a quota system, a system in effect from 1924 to 1965.

Immigrant reaction to the demand for assimilation took many forms, and is recorded in a large body of literature. Some turned inward and emphasized private experience.[5] Others - anarchists, socialists, communists - dreamed of and wrote about radically changing the society into which they had recently been admitted. Some (Jews, Negroes) thought of a new homeland to call their own. Most let themselves be assimilated as best they could. They were helped and often led by their own organizations. One of the groups most severely affected by racial prejudice and social Darwinism, the Jews, were also most active in creating organizations (B'nai Brith, Anti-Defamation League, American Jewish Committee, NAACP, Julius Rosenwald Fund) which would counteract not only antisemitism, but racial and anti-immigrant prejudice in general. The radicals sneered at them as reformists.

It was the Anti-Defamation League which supported one of the earliest studies of Puerto Rican immigration[6] to which we now turn.

Somehow, the Puerto Ricans escaped the social Darwinists and the eugenic planners. In 1917, when racist debates were at their most strident, and "science" had made even some dedicated liberals into adherents of racist views, the U. S. Congress enacted the Jones Law which granted American Citizenship to the Puerto Ricans. Probably the Jones Law meant little to the North Americans at the time. Only a few thousand Puerto Ricans were living on the mainland then. It is a safe guess that no one thought at the time that there would be a million of them in the nation's largest metropolitan area a few decades later, and that they would demand to be taken seriously as citizens and as human beings with a culture to be treated on a par with that of the Anglos.

All major Anglo students of Puerto Rican immigration had studied the history of prior immigration waves. By and large, they all predicted that sooner or later the "newcomers" would be assimilated as earlier newcomers had been. From what they had learned about history, they rather confidently predicted that history would repeat itself - with a few variations easily accommodated under catchall terms such as "cultural democracy" or "cultural pluralism". Thus Handlin states:

> ...the experience of the past offers a solid foundation for the
> belief that the newest immigrants to a great metropolitan city will
> come to play as useful a role in it as any of its predecessors.
> They themselves need only to show the will and energy and their
> neighbors the tolerance to make it possible.[7]

A little later, students began to express some doubts about assimilation. Senior even questioned whether it was desirable:

> Large numbers of our ancestors were placed in such a position by
> the "melting pot" school of "Americanism" and by other forms of
> rejection. Those who urged that the immigrant "forget the past"
> were asking the impossible - at least the undesirable.[8]

Yet the same author stresses that Puerto Ricans share many of the characteristics of prior immigrants:

> The "visible" Puerto Rican, especially when he is on or near the
> bottom of the economic ladder, has problems, just as other poor
> people have problems. There are no characteristic problems which
> the Puerto Rican has to carry alone; all that he has he shares with
> thousands of others in other ethnic groups, and they all share them
> with our ancestors.[9]

Senior then asserts that Puerto Ricans will be assimilated more rapidly than Blacks or Mexicans. He cites among other supportive pieces of evidence the numerous Puerto Rican business and professional organizations, the "substantial" enrollment of Puerto Ricans in the city's colleges and universities, and the dispersion of Puerto Ricans all over the city.[10]

A decade later, one becomes painfully aware of the cold fact that membership in business and professional organizations is small, that enrollment in higher education is disproportionately small and difficult to increase in spite of valiant efforts by Puerto Rican groups such as Aspira, and that the million Puerto Ricans have not dispersed much. The vast majority live in the few barrios allotted to them by their Anglo neighbors.

> ...that "unity with diversity" is the ideal of the democratic
> citizen of the United States, that just as violins or colorful
> threads make their contribution to a symphony or a tapestry, so
> the "strangers in a strange land" need not divest themselves of
> their culture heritage.[11]

Glazer and Moynihan[12] offer a series of essays on the five major ethnic minority groups of New York City. Their general assertion is that at least for those five groups the melting pot "did not happen".[13] In their predictions as to what will happen to the Puerto Ricans in New York, they seem rather uncertain. They project the emergence of four groups within which some older ethnic distinctions will be leveled: Catholics (Irish, Italian, Polish, German Catholics), Jewish (Ashkenazi and Sephardic), Negro (largely Protestant) and white Protestant Anglo-Saxon (Dutch, German, Scandinavian).[14] No telling where the Puerto Ricans will fit into this schema:

> In this large array of the four major religion-racial groups, where do
> the Puerto Ricans stand? Ultimately perhaps they are to be absorbed
> into the Catholic group. But that is a long time away. The Puerto
> Ricans are separated from the Catholics as well as the Negroes by
> color and culture. One cannot even guess how this large element will
> ultimately relate itself to the other elements of the city...[15]

But sure enough, the authors revert to the assimilationist stance within the very same sentence:

> ...perhaps it will serve, in line with its own nature and genius, to soften the sharp lines that divide them.[16]

The authors' hesitancy about predicting the Puerto Ricans' future may be realistic enough. But their assessment of the Puerto Rican background might make one think that the Puerto Ricans should, if anything, be submerged in the mainstream by the very lack of a strong identity of their own. They state that:

> The net of culture keeps up pride and encourages effort; the strong family serves to organize and channel resources in new situations.[17]

But they give the Puerto Ricans poor marks in both these critical areas. Their culture is said to be "weak in folk arts, unsure in its cultural tradition, without a powerful faith".[18] Documentation for these sweeping assertions is scant and clearly derived from readings (in English) as well as the authors' preconceived notions.[19]

In summary, we can say that North American observers tend to see Puerto Rican immigrants (and their island background) through their own cultural blinders. These include a strong tendency to stress the similarities to prior immigrations. Where differences are perceived, they are mostly seen as deficiencies. And the writers remain assimilationists at heart, perhaps inevitably so. They may be cautious in their predictions, as Glazer and Moynihan are, but the basic concern remains the same:

> ...the American nationality is still forming: its processes are mysterious, and the final form, if there ever is to be a final form, is as yet unknown.[20]

More recent observers of the New York developments have had to rethink some of the old assumptions. Ten years ago, Glazer and Moynihan could still say, perhaps correctly at the time, that young Puerto Rican leaders in New York saw their fellow countrymen as:

> ...following in the path of the earlier ethnic groups that preceded it, and (speak) of them as models for emulation rather than as targets for attack.[21]

Only a few years later, a North American with long and intimate knowledge of Puerto Ricans, Fitzpatrick, found it necessary to acknowledge that the militant pressures of the young generation were making themselves felt, creating a stressful relationship with the older generation, and more importantly a climate in which demands were formulated that went directly counter to the old assimilationist policies. Fitzpatrick still believes that assimilation will ultimately take place:

> The adjustment of Puerto Ricans to New York...is the continuation of an old experience among New Yorkers, but it is working itself out in very new ways. No particular theory of assimilation is adequate to analyze it.[22]

In our learning process within the project, much of which occurred in direct contact and sometimes in confrontation with individual Puerto Ricans and vocal professional or political groups, our own North American cultural blinders were repeatedly attacked. It seemed to us that even those who did not want independence for the Island were making demands which, if successfully pushed through, would create a true cultural pluralism. (We are not saying that this would be desirable, we are merely reporting our experience.

It may be that New York City at least will become a bilingual English-Hispanic community, and will remain so. This has never been granted to any group in any real sense before, but there are four major reasons for a type of resistance to assimilation which create a push toward such novel societal structures:

1) Language:

The Spanish language is not perceived by many Puerto Ricans, especially the young, as something to be unlearned, or to be kept at best as a relic of the past. It is to be given equal status to English. Schools with predominantly Puerto Rican enrollment are to be fully bilingual. City employees are to be fluent in Spanish - or at least each city agency is to have bilingual personnel on hand. What is being asked is considerably more than the occasional multi-lingualism with which the City is familiar, and which occurs primarily when some political advantage is to be gained (we have seen voter instructions and political fliers printed in four languages: Spanish, Yiddish, Chinese and English).[23]

2) Attitudes toward Race

Racial mixture is to become an accepted pattern for those who intermarry. This is what our laws ("stateways") say should be done. Of course, our customs and attitudes ("folkways") are very far from such acceptance. Allport's[24] hope that Sumner's dictum, "stateways follow folkways" could be reversed, has not come true, and may not for a long time to come.[25]

3) Proximity of the Island

The earlier immigrants' break with the homeland was final for the majority of them. The Puerto Rican pattern is strikingly different. The proximity of the Island and cheap airfares have made the Puerto Rican immigration a "commuter migration". Contact with the old culture is far more immediate and continuous than anything earlier immigrants had. There is no faraway old country to dream of, but a living culture of which the New York Puerto Rican is an integral part. Furthermore, the homeland is not a foreign country. It is, in its odd way, part of the United States. And this leads to what may be the single most important reason why Puerto Rican resistance to assimilation may be more successful than similar resistances in the past.

4) Citizenship

In order to understand the Puerto Rican attitude toward citizenship (ambivalent though it may be), it is useful to go back to the meaning of citizenship for the North American, and for non-Puerto Rican immigrants. Immigration to North America is not a right. It is a privilege granted by Congress, one that has been prized by millions who fled from religious, racial or political persecution, and by many who simply sought economic betterment. The immigration procedures are quite lengthy and complex, and are based on the assumption that the immigrant will wish to become a citizen. Naturalization requires additional qualifications including years of continuous residence, reasonable literacy in English and some knowledge of U. S. institutions. The F.B.I. checks to find out whether the applicant has had trouble with the law and is of good moral character. The would-be American must solemnly promise under oath to renounce all past allegiances and to be a good citizen.[26]

But now look at the Puerto Ricans. We stated above that, to the North American, he is an immigrant, part of yet another wave when there had been so many before. We claimed that to the North American, the Puerto Rican's citizenship status was a mere technicality resulting from some historical accident many years ago. The popular expectation remains that he should learn "the" language, forget his Island past, and become just like us as fast as he can. If he makes honest efforts in this direction, we may eventually accept him as a neighbor, and even learn to appreciate those diversities which are not threatening to our unity. To the Puerto Rican, all of this is deeply offensive. Citizenship is his birthright; no one may ask him to prove himself worthy of it. The Island is part of the United States, and not a faraway place belonging to a past which is best forgotten. And last but not least his language is the one which he learned as an American citizen. He may be quite willing to learn English as a second language in order to advance himself, but the idea of having to learn it in order to prove he is a good citizen is insulting.

It is these two viewpoints, the North American and the Puerto Rican, which are in conflict, and this conflict may be more important than the one around the political status of the Island. Puerto Ricans certainly do not see themselves as refugees, and certainly not as members of a "defective" culture. The very fact of their citizenship gives them the rationale and perhaps in time the political power to change one thing which North Americans have taken for granted throughout the history of the nation: that assimilation is not only inevitable (which indeed it may be), but that it is the only desirable goal.

Footnotes:

1. H. Hapgood. The Spirit of the Ghetto (1902). New York: Schocken, 1966. Foreward.

2. Marqués, op. cit., p. 171. (our translation)

        Doña Gariela: I don't want them to bury him in this
                                         land without sun. Will it take much to
                                       take him to Puerto Rico?

        Juanita: Never mind how much it will cost.

3. Joseph P. Fitzpatrick, op. cit., p. 35.

4. R. Hofstadter, Social Darwinism in American Thought, revised edition. (Boston: Beacon Press, 1955), p. 162.

5. H. Roth, op. cit.

6. C. Senior. The Puerto Ricans: Strangers, then Neighbors. (Chicago: Quadrangle Books, 1965).

7. Oscar Handlin. The Newcomers. (Cambridge, Mass.: Harvard University Press, 1959), p.121.

8. Senior, op. cit., p. 59.

9. Ibid., p. 43.

10. Ibid., pp. 98-100

11. Ibid., p. 62

12. N. Glazer and D. Moynihan. Beyond the Melting Pot. (Cambridge, Mass.: M.I.T. Press, 1963).

13. Ibid., p. v.

14. Ibid., p. 314.

15. Ibid., p. 315.

16. Ibid., p. 315

17. Ibid., p. 88.

18. Ibid., op. cit., p. 88.

19. How little they observe the usual canons of social science can be illustrated by the following examples:

      Even Puerto Rican Spiritualism, while it owed something to traits
      borrowed from Haiti and Cuba (and thus indirectly from Africa),
      seemed to be based more directly on the works of a nineteenth-
      century French writer on occult matters. (Glazer and Moynihan, p. 88)

This statement deserves a closer look because of its implied value assumptions. Apparently cultural borrowing, especially if it is "indirect" is an indicator of weakness. Yet all but the most remote and isolated cultures have thrived on such borrowing. Europeans often view all things American as "merely" derivative of the expressions of one or the other of their own various ethnics. And why should using a minor French writer as a lender be worse than using original ancient African tribal rites? To anyone seriously concerned with cross-cultural communication, such value judgments are objectionable. And to anyone who bothers to learn about the importance to Puerto Ricans of _espiritismo_ in all social classes, such judgments are an indicator of ignorance or lack of scholarly discipline.

In the second critical area, family stability, the authors stress the frequency of consensual marriage and the break-up of such marriages (Glazer and Moynihan, p. 89). And they dutifully list one of the strong autochtonous institutions which Puerto Ricans and other Latin Americans developed to a degree unknown in Europe; godparenthood (compadrazgo) (p. 90). But no sooner have we become duly alarmed about children growing up in "confused family settings" (p. 89) that we are told children are loved and "overprotected" (p. 90). If Glazer and Moynihan were writing about Polynesian islanders, they might have been more careful. It is quite possible that family arrangements which were adequate for the rural island culture become inadequate as that culture is confronted with industrialization. It is possible that customary arrangements through the extended family and the godparents may not serve well on the mainland. But all this is a matter of empirical observation, and should not be decided by the _fiat_ of prior value assumptions.

20. _Ibid._, _op_. _cit_., p. 315.

21. _Ibid._, p. 128

22. Fitzpatrick, _op_. _cit_., p. 184

23. Recently, a federal court has supported an agreement between the New York City Board of Education and Aspira. This will result in a pilot program of bilingual education affecting no less than 40 local schools from the elementary to the high school level. The two features of the pilot program which are most significant in the contest of our discussion are:

    1. Intensive teaching of English as a _second_ language to Puerto Ricans and other Hispanics (our emphasis).

    2. Teaching of the regular curriculum in Spanish and reinforcing (reforzar) the use of Spanish in order to produce students who can _function in Spanish._

    Both these features seem to imply an intent to give the Spanish language a standing which no other language has ever had in the New York City Public School System.

    "Anker Nombra 40 Escuelas Daran Instruccion Bilingue." _El Diario_. November 6, 1974, p. 2.

24. G. W. Allport. _The Nature of Prejudice_ (1954). (New York: Doubleday; Anchor Books, 1958), p. 437f.

25. The Puerto Rican attitude toward race is complex, and has been described often. A good summary can be found in Fitzpatrick (_op_. _cit_., pp. 101-104). An analysis of the issue claiming a radical difference between North American and Puerto Rican

attitudes toward race is offered by Seda Bonilla (<u>Requiem por una cultura.</u>
Rio Piedras, P.R.: Editorial Edie, 1970.) pp. 39-76.

26. Many, of course, would forget the past if only they could. One of us who was
a participant in such an industion ceremony saw quite a few of his new fellow
Americans in tears - of sorrow for a lost homeland? of relief at liberation from
past threats? of gratitude for being accepted into the new community?

CHAPTER 7

SOCIAL PROBLEMS AND MENTAL HEALTH

Social Problems and Pathology Which Led to this Project

The orientation of social work and mental health professionals is toward social problems or social pathology - i.e., conditions which should be alleviated or behavioral patterns which should be cured or at least ameliorated. The social problems and pathology which suggested our project were:

1. The tremendous increase in narcotic drug abuse in the United States. This increase was felt most strongly in the New York metropolitan area, where about one-half of the nation's drug abusers were said to be located. A disproportionately large number of users were said to be Puerto Rican.[1] This social belief whether or not based on fact fitted well into the pattern of suspicion and fear that is an important part of the social perception of Puerto Ricans in New York.

2. In response to the perceived need, the number of social work and medical agencies serving drug abusers increased by leaps and bounds, until there were over 300 such agencies in 1973.[2]

3. There had been an increasing awareness of the difficulties of Puerto Rican clients in using social service agencies.[3]

Some of these difficulties were cultural. A Puerto Rican, when in need of help tried to use the familiar pattern of help-seeking he had learned on the Island. He might try to turn to the extended family, or to ritual kin (compadres). He might even try to rely on the island value of personalismo, that is, he might try to turn to his employer.[4] Perhaps the last place he would turn to was an anonymous social agency, especially if it required traveling far from home and enduring the fearful experience of using a subway.[5]

Some of these difficulties were simply that the doctor or social worker did not speak Spanish. Not only could he not be trusted to understand the cultural background of the client, but he just did not understand what the client was trying to say.

Puerto Ricans as an Underclass

Twenty years ago, Mintz stated:

The biggest, most publicized, and most important migration of Puerto Ricans has been that to New York City. While not immigrants by legal definition, since Puerto Ricans are United States citizens and can enter and leave the mainland freely, the significant differences between United States culture and Puerto Rican culture, including that of language, the relative lack of knowledge that Puerto Ricans and North Americans have of one another, and the fact that most Puerto Ricans move into both metropolitan and farm areas as unskilled laborers filling jobs that other Americans are avoiding, (our emphasis) combine to make this migration similar to that of previous large-scale migrations from other lands to the United States.[6]

48

Mintz correctly describes an immigration pattern which has been true for a century and a half and into which the Puerto Ricans fit rather well. We noted above the major distinction that Puerto Ricans are American citizens, whether we like it or not, and that this fact makes for a difference in attitude on the part of the immigrants if not of their North American hosts. Another distinction is that Puerto Rican immigration to the mainland was for a time systematically encouraged by the island government as one way of dealing with the overpopulation problem retaining skilled workers and "exporting" unskilled laborers has been a matter of policy.

For the North Americans, then, Puerto Ricans were a familiar problem: an underclass of poor, unskilled people, unfamiliar with "the" language, and ready to accept the menial jobs which the natives or the more assimilated would no longer take on.

Over the years, the Puerto Ricans have improved their occupational positions (again following a familiar pattern). Fitzpatrick[7] notes these changes as they were reflected in the 1950 and 1960 census data: both men and women have moved on to more skilled and better-paying jobs.

In spite of these improvements, Puerto Ricans as a group still constitute an underclass primarily employed in the restaurant and garment trades. They are still poor - and thus the recipients of the benevolent attention of those professionally engaged in tending to the poor.

Puerto Ricans and Mental Illness

Back in 1956, Malzberg[8] studied mental disease among Puerto Ricans who had come to the mainland in 1949-51. He found that the incidence of schizophrenia was more than twice as high for Puerto Rican men than for the general population: 105 per 100,000 vs. 45.4 per 100,000. Fitzpatrick[9] reports an even greater contrast: "The rate of first admissions for schizophrenia for Puerto Rican males in New York State in 1967 was 122 per 100,000, whereas the rate for males in the general population was 36.6..."

Let us accept these diagnoses as correct for the sake of discussion.[10] If a schizophrenia rate twice as high was bad in 1956, obviously a rate three times as high in 1967 is worse. Was not Malzberg then correct in warning us of the consequences of Puerto Rican mass immigration, one of which would be an increase in psychiatric disorder? After all, is this not what has happened? And is it not now a social fact that Puerto Ricans are more prone to schizophrenic reactions?

But before we accept this as a social fact, perhaps we should remind ourselves that if 122 per 100,000 Puerto Ricans are indeed schizophrenic, this also does mean that 99,878 per 100,000 are not. And that may be the most important social fact to remember in our attempts to define the social situation of Puerto Ricans in New York City.

A second major example of how a minor social science finding can be transmogrified into social fact is offered by the justly famous Midtown Manhattan Study.[11] This epidemiological study was an attempt to examine mental health and illness in a section of Manhattan. Few Puerto Ricans lived there at the time, so the sampling procedures used in the study "caught" only 27 Puerto Ricans, who were interviewed along with over 1600 others.

The Puerto Ricans in the sample seem to be problem people indeed. Few of them are mentally "well". In fact, of the 23 first-generation Puerto Ricans, not a single one is "well", and more than half are "impaired", meaning that they show marked to severe mental health symptom formation.[12]

The authors of the Midtown Manhattan Study are very careful in labeling their comments as speculations.[13] The two most important speculations are the following:

1. The Puerto Ricans tend to be strongly attached to their ethnic group. This is not very surprising since most of them are recent arrivals. In a somewhat perilous inferential leap, the authors suggest that group attachment does not go well with mental health, or, in their own words: "Seemingly intimated here is the existence of some sort of relationship between ethnic detachment and wellness."[14]

2. The Puerto Ricans' poor mental health status did not seem to be only a correlate of their low socio-economic status. Rather, they were a small number of isolates scattered among a large non-Puerto Rican population. In fact, they might even have chosen to live outside of the barrio precisely because they had mental health problems to begin with which made them misfits with their own kind.[15] In effect, the authors of the study properly stress the severe eccentricity of their small sample, and warn the reader away from careless generalization.

But once a social scientist has gone into print, his findings are what is remembered, and the qualifications with which he has hedged them are forgotten. And so, these 27 Puerto Rican New Yorkers have had a minor career in the sociological and psychiatric literature.

Predictably, they turn up in Glazer and Moynihan. The authors quote Malzberg on the high rates of Puerto Rican admission to mental hospitals, and go on to say:

> And the Midtown Study of mental health showed a remarkably high rate
> of impairment for the Puerto Ricans in the East Midtown area. This
> is not one of the typical areas of Puerto Rican settlement; the
> authors suggest that this group, isolated from the main body of new
> migrants, may be under greater strain than Puerto Ricans in more
> characteristically Puerto Rican parts of the city, yet the findings
> are consistent with other findings on rates of illness (our emphasis).
> The migration it seems has hit New York Puerto Ricans very hard.[16]

Now, these "other findings" are mainly, once more, Malzberg, and a study focusing primarily on the physical health of a sample of 80 Puerto Rican families.[17] And our 27 Puerto Rican expatriates are now presented in such a way as to confirm the average North American's social perception of all Puerto Ricans as problem people.

Later writers on Puerto Rican matters[18] mention the Midtown Manhattan Study in passing, mainly in reference to their concern with the correlation between social class and mental illness. By and large, they leave the 27 East Side Puerto Ricans alone.

In 1971, however, Fitzpatrick chose to resurrect the poor fellows. In his discussion of the Midtown Manhattan Study, he states:

> There were 27 Puerto Ricans in the sample, and they came off far worse
> than any other ethnic group. Poverty was not found to be a signifi-
> cant factor; the study supported the hypothesis of isolation.[19]

No doubt the statement is technically correct. But the key issues: the smallness of the sample, and its non-representativeness, are not likely to be noticed by even a reasonably careful reader. What he will remember is that, once more, the Puerto Ricans "came off far worse."

We have followed the literary career of the Midtown Manhattan Study Puerto Ricans in some detail because these 27 men have been presented so many times and in so many contexts by colleagues and students and because especially the latter had to be reminded time and time again to be wary of social perceptions which confirm rather than challenge what they take to be accepted knowledge.

Perhaps the hapless Puerto Ricans caught, rather accidentally, in the sampling net of the Midtown Manhattan Study interviewers should be laid to rest once and for all. For there are a million or so Puerto Ricans to be observed. Few of them are schizophrenic. Undoubtedly some are sick. Some may be well, and perhaps most of them are a little bit of both, as are most human beings.

Puerto Ricans and the Culture of Poverty

Our third major example of the manufacture of social facts from questionable findings is the work of Oscar Lewis, and specifically his concept of a culture of poverty. The study of most immediate interest is, of course, La Vida[20], because it deals with the life of some people not only in San Juan, but also in New York.

The concept of a culture of poverty has been the object of much attention from admirers and critics. It has influenced the social thought and social action of the sixties. Harrington[21] used it extensively, and Lewis somewhat plaintively states that that use was "in a somewhat broader and less technical sense than I had intended."[22]

It is most important to note here (in fairness to Lewis and his readers) that La Vida was meant to be only the first in a series of volumes on the culture of poverty concept as he had developed it shortly before his premature death.[23]

Theoretical Perspectives

Let us recall here the main theoretical perspectives on the culture of poverty as stated by Lewis:

1) the culture of poverty in its relation to the larger society: It is characterized by a "lack of effective participation and integration of the poor in the major institutions of the larger society..."[24]

2) the nature of the slum community: There is "a minimum of organization beyond the level of the nuclear and the extended family."[25]

3) the family level: The absence of middle class mores is presented in a long list ranging from absence of childhood to early sex, unstable marriage and "a strong predisposition to authoritarianism."[26]

4) the individual level: Here again the list of traits, most of them valued as defective, is long. We go from sociological notions of marginality to psychoanalytic notions "of maternal deprivation, of orality, of weak ego structure, confusion of sexual identification, a lack of impulse control, a strong present-time orientation with relatively little ability to defer gratification and to plan for the future, a sense of resignation and fatalism, a widespread belief in male superiority, and a high tolerance for psychological pathology of all sorts."[27]

This is quite a list of cultural and psychological traits. Perhaps they are all deplorable, especially from a middle class standpoint. But some traits, especially the more psychologically oriented ones, sound suspiciously familiar as the usual catalog of moral sins translated into the language of mental health.

The fact that the Rios family, whose history and day-to-day life is presented so vividly and directly, is part of a very skewed, unrepresentative sample has been noted by many critics.[28]

The Rios family comes from a San Juan slum which is in itself different from other Puerto Rican urban slums; the women living in La Esmeralda (located near the port and tourist areas) are more often involved in prostitution than are the women of other slums; the women of the Rios family conform much less to the cultural norm of female submissiveness than do other Puerto Rican women.

Lewis' own disclaimer of representativeness should be noted: "...the data should not be generalized to Puerto Rican society as a whole. Much of the behavior described in these pages goes counter to some of the most cherished ideals of the larger society."[29]

No doubt Lewis' best justification for his method is the emphasis on the range of variation within a culture as opposed to the emphasis on total configurations.[30]

As long as one remembers the eccentricity of the Rios family, one may well use it to gain an oblique glance at the larger Puerto Rican and New York Puerto Rican society, somewhat in the same sense in which pathological thought can be used to gain insight into normal thought. But the danger that we may think of the Rios as "the" Puerto Ricans is ever-present, and Lewis' own ambiguity on the subject does not help.

Social Disorganization

Lewis' concept of a culture of poverty is perhaps best defined as an attempt at describing social disorganization and marginality under conditions or rapid culture change. From this perspective, he also searches for regularities across cultures rather than a mere description of variants within a culture. Note, however, that he stressed the need "to test and refine" the concept.[31]

His own comparison of Mexicans and Puerto Ricans in the culture of poverty almost inevitably gets him involved in rather broad generalizations, including ones in which Puerto Ricans are presented as culturally inferior. For instance, "in Mexico even the poorest slum dwellers have a much richer sense of the past and a deeper identification with the Mexican tradition than do Puerto Ricans with their tradition."[32] No substantive data are presented to support this assertion.

This is only one example where Lewis' cultural value positions show through without being examined. Cultural stability, anchored in family, religion and tradition (the older the better) are obviously highly valued. Cultural change is viewed with suspicion and fear (except when it is defined as "progressive", i. e., socialist). He tries to locate the culture of poverty in a setting of political economy: it is an adaptation to a "class-stratified, highly individuated, capitalistic society." And it most frequently "develops when a stratified social and economic system is breaking down or is being replaced by another." No doubt there is merit in these sweeping historical perspectives, and a good deal of supportive evidence could be adduced by many. But the theme of social disorganization as the key characteristic of the culture of poverty is questioned by Lewis himself, in examples of groups who do not fit the definition. Many quite poor primitive peoples have a "relatively integrated, satisfying and self-sufficient culture." The caste organization of India "gives individuals a sense of identify and belonging." The poor Jews of eastern Europe had a tradition of literacy, a community organized around the rabbi, a "proliferation of voluntary associations", and their religion.[37]

But one cannot help but feel that Lewis' interest is in individuals rather than a broad socio-economic framework. Hence the focus on intensive family studies, and on family and individual psychodynamics. He seems to like people rather more than social-scientific abstractions.

For instance, he claims that "the precipitating factor for leaving Puerto Rico was "most often a personal socio-psychological crisis."[38] This is in contrast to the fairly generally held view that the major reason for migration is the hope for economic betterment.[39] And when he finds that the income of his 50 New York Puerto Rican sample families is three to four times higher than that of his 100 San Juan sample families, he does not dwell on the notion that Puerto Ricans might know that in New York one can make more money.[40] Rather, he moves on quickly to describe how the Rios' had spent an inordinate proportion of their New York income on clothes and jewelry.

Social Reorganization

If the correct diagnosis for the members of the culture of poverty is social and personal disorganization, the prescription obviously is one of social and personal reorganization. Lewis moves this again into his personalistic focus. For the developed countries in which allegedly only a small segment of the population lives in the culture of poverty as defined, reformist measures are noted without disapproval:

> In the United States, the major solutions proposed by planners and social workers in dealing with multiple-problem families and the so-called hard-core of poverty has been to attempt slowly to raise their level of living and to incorporate them into the middle class. Wherever possible, there has been some reliance upon psychiatric treatment.[41]

For underdeveloped countries, where "psychiatrists can hardly begin to cope" with the magnitude of the problem, revolution may be the correct prescription. "Revolutions frequently succeed in abolishing some of the basic characteristics of the culture of poverty even when they do not succeed in abolishing poverty itself."[42] The revolution should be socialist, of course: "I am inclined to believe that the culture of poverty does not exist in socialist countries."[43]

Lewis' romantic, person-oriented view of social reorganization is clearly an echo of early 19th century socialism, and very much in tune with the social movements of the sixties, whether reformist or radical. His view implies a faith in human nature and its perfectibility which has an obvious appeal to people professionally engaged in intervening with humans. Thus, if ultimately the problem of the culture of poverty can be used to giving priority to changing a person's consciousness, the professional is quite at home with his familiar methods of intervention, even if he technically switches from reorganizing individuals or families to reorganizing "communities".

What Lewis did for us and many others was to focus our attention on those for whom ultimately all social changes are supposed to take place, and all stable social orders are to exist: people. In presenting the Rios family, he has shown us some of the "wrong" people of Puerto Rico and New York. In this sense, he may have helped to manufacture social facts by making many believe that all Puerto Ricans are like the Rios'. Perhaps the "right" people are different in many respects.

An attempt to present Puerto Rican social service clients in the context of the Puerto Rican rather than the Anglo value system was made by Minuchin and his group.[44]

In their study, twelve "experimental" families were under intensive scrutiny. Most were living on welfare, and all had produced delinquent children who had been placed in the care of a residential treatment center. Two of these families were Puerto Rican.[45] Ten "control" families were also observed. They differed from the "experimental" families in that their children were not delinquent. Most of them were also living on welfare. They further differed from the "experimental" families in that they were not given treatment.[46] Two of these "control" families were Puerto Rican.[47] We are dealing once again with a small and eccentric sample of welfare clients living in ghettos, some of whom produced delinquent children.

In a frankly speculative section, the authors use this sample and unspecified other interventions with Puerto Ricans to develop a composite portrait of their Puerto Rican families.[48] The chief merit of this attempt is that they contrast their disorganized client families with what they believe to be a more typical Puerto Rican family organization. They stress the capacity of the organized, though poor, family for affective interplay as opposed to the disorganized families' interactions which are said to be built upon "enmeshed exchanges revolving around violence, sex and money".[49] Values and role expectations such as manliness (machismo), respect (respeto), and female exploitedness and submissiveness are described, and a perceptive analysis of the spiritist beliefs (espiritismo) as a "protective framework of externalization"[50] is offered.

What makes this short section so useful for the student of Puerto Ricans is that, for a change, we find a stress on the strengths of the Puerto Rican culture rather than its presumed weaknesses. The authors also suggest that even the disorganized families have some access to Puerto Rican cultural traditions, so that the latter provide an orienting frame of reference.[51] This careful characterization is far from idealizing Puerto Ricans; it is noteworthy because of the absence of negative stereotypes we have found so often in the literature, and which so clearly reflected the unexamined assumptions of the Anglo observer. Possibly the fact that the two senior authors were not only fluent in Spanish but also grew up in a Spanish-speaking culture[52] had something to do with this attitude. This lends some credence to the demands of Puerto Rican social workers that more Spanish-speaking and indigenous personnel is needed.[53]

After this long excursion into diagnoses of psychopathology and the culture of poverty, and a variety of prescriptions ranging from social psychiatry to world revolution, perhaps it is only fair to note that the single most perceptive description of social and family life among poor New York Puerto Ricans was given by a Puerto Rican anthropologist whose work predated most of the studies cited in this section. This is Padilla's Up from Puerto Rico.[54] It seems to us that after all the changes of the last 15 years, her level-headed account is as fresh and relevant as anything that has been offered since then.

Footnotes:

1. Fitzpatrick, op. cit., pp. 170-178.

2. I. Weisman and F. S. Schwartz (eds.). Directory of Services for the Drug Abuser and Addict in New York City. (New York: Hunter College School of Social Work and New York City Addiction Services Agency, 1972).

3. C. Garcia. Study of the Initial Involvement in the Social Services by the Puerto Rican Migrants in Philadelphia. (Philadelphia: Vantage Press, 1971). D. Tendler. Social Service Needs in a Changing Community: A Study of the use of Voluntary Social Agencies by Puerto Rican Clients. Unpublished Doctoral dissertation. (New York: New York University, 1965).

4. M. M. Jones. Villa Flores: A Community's Attitudes Toward Welfare. Unpublished M.S.W. thesis. (New York: Hunter College School of Social Work, 1973).

5. L. Podell. Families on Welfare in New York City. (New York: CUNY Center for the Study of Urban Problems, n.d.), pp. xxiif.

6. S. W. Mintz. "Puerto Rican Emigration: a Threefold Comparison". Social and Economic Studies, Vol. 4, No. 4 (December, 1955). Reprinted in Fernández Méndez (ed.) Portrait of a Society. (Rio Piedras, P.R.: University of Puerto Rico Press, 1972), pp. 219-232.

7. Fitzpatrick, op. cit., p. 61.

8. B. Malzberg. "Mental Disease Among Puerto Ricans in New York City, 1949-51", Journal of Nervous and Mental Disease, Vol. 123 (1956), 457-465.

9. Fitzpatrick, op. cit., p. 162.

10. Whether or not they really are is a matter that needs careful exploration. Fitzpatrick, suggested the possibility that Puerto Ricans may be "treated for mental illnesses which they do not have." (p. 162)

11. L. Srole, et. al. Mental Health in the Metropolis. New York: McGraw-Hill, 1962.

12. Ibid., p. 291.

13. Ibid., p. 293.

14. Ibid, p. 293.

15. Ibid., p. 291.

16. Glazer and Moynihan op. cit., p. 122.

17. B. Berle. Eighty Puerto Rican Families in New York City. (New York: Columbia University Press, 1959).

18. L. H. Rogler, and August Hollingshead. Trapped: Families and Schizophrenia. (New York: Wiley, 1965). B. P. Dohrenwend, and B. S. Dohrenwend. Social Status and Psychological Disorder. (New York: Wiley-Interscience, 1969).

19. Fitzpatrick, op. cit., p. 165.

20. Oscar Lewis. _La Vida_. (New York: Vintage Books, 1965).

21. M. Harrington. _The Other America_. (New York: Macmillan, 1963).

22. Lewis, _op. cit._, p. xiii.

23. _Ibid._, p. xviii.

24. _Ibid._, p. xiv.

25. _Ibid._, p. xivi.

26. _Ibid._, p. xicii.

27. _Ibid._, p. xiviii.

28. G. S. Goldberg and E. W. Gordon, "La Vida: Whose Life?" _IRCD Bulletin_, Vol. 4, No. 1 (1968).

29. Lewis, _op. cit._, p. xiii.

30. _Ibid._, p. xv.

31. _Ibid._, p. xviii.

32. _Ibid._, p. xvii.

33. _Ibid._, p. xliv.

34. _Ibid._, p. lv, p. xlv.

35. _Ibid._, p. xlviii.

36. _Ibid._, p. xlix.

37. _Ibid._, p. xlix.

38. _Ibid._, p. xxxviii.

39. Fitzpatrick, _op. cit._

40. Lewis, _op. cit._, p. xxxix.

41. _Ibid._, p. lii.

42. _Ibid._, p. lii.

43. _Ibid._, p. xlix.

44. S. Minuchin, _et. al_. _Families in the Slums_. (New York: Basic Books, 1967).

45. _Ibid._, pp. 7, 388.

46. _Ibid._ p. 8

47. _Ibid._, p. 7, 388.

48. _Ibid._, pp. 237-242.

49. _Ibid._, p. 237.

50. _Ibid._, p. 241.

51. _Ibid._, p. 237.

52. _Ibid._, p. x.

53. Council on Social Work Education. _The Puerto Rican People: A Selected Bibliography for Use in Social Work Education._ (New York: Council on Social Work Education, 1973), p. ix.

54. E. Padilla. _Up from Puerto Rico._ (New York: Columbia University Press, 1968).

CHAPTER 8

THE CROSS CULTURAL PROJECT WITH PUERTO RICO

In the beginning, the project was conceived as an exchange program, with Hunter College School of Social Work graduate students going to San Juan Puerto Rico for one semester and University of Puerto Rico School of Social Work graduate students coming to New York for one semester. The major method for learning the culture was to be through the field work experience.

The Puerto Rican students were generally quite fluent in English. It had been originally assumed that with some language training in New York City prior to coming to Puerto Rico, the New York students would begin their field work experience as observers with bi-lingual Puerto Rican students. Then they would be assigned to bi-lingual clients for direct experience, and as their language skills improved they would take on Spanish-speaking individuals and groups to work with. The plan was too difficult to carry out in three months - the number of adjustments in culture, climate and setting made the period a most demanding one.

What emerged was the recognition that the conventional social work field work model was not suitable for training in another language and culture. However, the field work experience could be reorganized so that similar goals could be achieved in New York.

It became clear that students coming from New York to Puerto Rico with modest language skills should come as learners rather than as practitioners. The goals of helping Anglo social workers to work with Puerto Rican people would be better achieved by a program that would place greater emphasis on language and the customs and traditions of the people.[1]

The Catholic University of Puerto Rico Training Center had a program which seemed to be well related to the needs of the Hunter College School of Social Work students. The Puerto Rico Training Center had for a number of years been the center for training in language and culture for the Peace Corps for Puerto Rico, Central America and South America. In addition, it trained personnel for industrial firms active in Latin America. A conference with the Director of the agency and his major staff members made it clear that they were interested and quite adaptable in their outlook.

The current training philosophy of the Center is that of Facilitated Learning.

Definition

Facilitated Learning is a concept which involves the trainee's using to the fullest extent all of his learning senses - vision, hearing, touch, smell, pain, etc. in both structured and spontaneous learning experiences. This must be done in such a way as to best achieve the development of those skills and attitudes essential to serving as an effective agent of change in his country of assignment. Behaviorial change in terms of specific skill development, rather than the passing on of a given body of knowledge, is the meaning of the training which results from the application of the concept of Facilitated Learning. Facilitated Learning, thus, has all of the elements of the experiential learning model with the added dimension of the trainer, or facilitator, who provides structure and sequence.

Based on the approach to learning defined above, we have developed the following set of assumptions regarding learning. It is upon these learning assumptions that our training is built:

Learning Assumptions

Assumption #1 - Learning takes place best for North American trainees when there is an emotional involvement followed by a cognitive understanding.

Assumption #2 - The ambience in which North Americans are trained for service with Latin Americans must be culturally distinct from the culture from which the trainee comes, and at times even hostile.

Assumption #3 - Within the ambience outlined in the previous assumptions, there must be a training institution which effectively carried out the following functions:

- provides materials and opportunities for cognitive learning together with skill development in the areas of language, cross-cultural communications and technical training.

- facilitates the trainee's learning experiences in the barrio, within Ponce's institutions and elsewhere on the Island.

- offers modeling for behavior which is appropriate to the on-the-job situation for which the trainee is preparing himself or herself.

- provides counselling and other assistance to the trainee as he goes through the process of adaptation to the 3rd culture.

- expands the experience of the individual by providing opportunities for him to share experiences within the learning community, both with his trainers and his peers.

- recognizes the need to attend to individual needs and learning styles.

Assumption #4 - North American trainees best adapt to a new cultural environment through a step-by-step, logically developed learning process. Thus, there is a need for proper sequencing of the appropriate learning experiences.[2]

The language program was 300 hours for a twelve week period (25 hours of language per 40 hour week). The staff ratio was one language teacher for every five students, one training assistant for every 10 students, and additional supervisory personnel. The language program is an adaptation of the State Department's Foreign Service training system and emphasizes situational reinforcement. The method of instruction has been proved with hundreds of Peace Corps trainees. The staff was prepared to start with persons with limited knowledge of Spanish who were interested and motivated. The objective for the 300 hundred hours of language training in the twelve week period was to develop in an individual sufficient knowledge of the language to converse freely and to interview in the language. In addition to their prepared texts, the Center would prepare appropriate manuals using social welfare and drug abuse terms that were necessary for working in the drug abuse field in Spanish.

Basic to the entire program of the Puerto Rico Training Center was their "live-in" arrangement. Each participating student for the entire twelve week period was required to live with a family in the barrio. The homes had been selected and some had been used over a period of time and were within thirty minutes travel time from the Training Center. All students were required to use public transportation with no private vehicles permitted. Thus, students were required to mingle with local residents in all aspects of their daily life.

The history and culture components which this Center used in the program followed the general development taken by Father Joseph Fitzpatrick in his 1971 book Puerto Rican Americans. 3 The Catholic University anthropologists and sociologists participated in this phase of the program. Language and culture were learned through academic instruction, plus the live-in experience in the barrio; the language of the specific field of interest, in this instance social work and drug abuse, was provided through the "work-in" experience, involving participant observation and direct practice in local agencies.

The "work-in" phase of the program consisted of twelve hours per week of participant observation in the special area of interest, drug abuse services, for three weeks. In the last three weeks of the twelve week period, each student had direct practice, three afternoons a week. Thus, we had a modified program of social work field work.

It might be possible to involve students in the life of the barrio and to simulate some of the experience in New York City, but it is very difficult to go through the acculturation process where one's escape to the familiar, comfortable world of one's own culture is but a short subway or bus trip away.

The Learning Center, which had a number of years of experience in preparing North Americans, Peace Corps volunteers, to live and work in the Hispanic world offered a model that could be translated to social work education.

Barrio Living

Living in the barrio helped the students to understand and adapt to Puerto Rican culture. The important learning tool in the barrio is the people. The students become aware of the customs, cultural clues, formalities and activities which help them understand and become sensitive to the Puerto Rican culture. The students begin to understand that all people (including themselves) are products of their own culture. In trying to accomplish this culture adaptation, the students must spend time with their Puerto Rican family and friends and participate as much as possible in family-related activities both in the home and in the community. Many cultural activities enhanced the barrio learning: attending weddings, mass, funerals, family parties, domino games, and patron festivities. Since the students were there in December, they participated in all of the exciting holiday preparations.

A barrio trainer was assigned to each student to help facilitate the students' interpretation of what they were experiencing, and to be available in case of problems. The trainers were Puerto Rican and in our frame of reference would be called paraprofessionals.

Implications for Social Work

The Puerto Rican population coming to New York City is a population in transition. For people in transition, their traditional culture is real, but the influence of the traditional culture is severely strained in the confrontation with the new dominant culture. The response of the client to such a confrontation is frequently appropriate from the perspective of the traditional culture, while inappropriate, perhaps even dysfunctional, from the perspective of the dominant culture. To be a male is different in different societies. What looks like deviant behavior may be coping behavior. Viktor Frankel observes that an abnormal reaction to an abnormal situation is normal behavior.[4]

Some of the contradictions that arise out of this transitional state, and which can cause difficulties which social work agencies must deal with, include:

1. The traditional system of relationships based on social class and family status and an industrial system based on personal competition, initiative, and conspicuous consumption as a basis for status.

2. High aspirations and low achievements.

3. Importance of dignity, pride and honor and the increasing emphasis on material wealth and consumption.

4. Value system that reveres the iibaro*, and that which reveres the successful entrepreneur.

5. The present commitment to democracy and the traditional methods of power that prevailed in the colonial system.[5]

Institutional policies often represent an inhospitable environment for minority persons who must adjust to the institutions' expectations if they are to establish and maintain their eligibility for service.

The difficulties related to a meeting of two cultures are not only those of the client population, but they are also difficulties of the social worker.

The worker has to understand the cultural values of the individual or family in treatment, to be able to assess the health or pathology in terms of that culture's norms as well as the norms of the dominant culture. The worker also needs to better understand the clients' conflicts.

Unless the worker is aware of the dominant American values which he has incorporated, as well as the values of his own family of origin, the worker may wittingly or unwittingly influence the treatment, e.g., the Puerto Rican man who was considered psychotic and violent because he beat his 16 year old daughter for staying out until 2:00 in the morning, and because he received messages from the spirits. Only the inadvertant intervention by another worker, more familiar with the culture, prevented this man from being hospitalized.

Social workers, while consciously becoming aware of the socio-cultural factors influencing the life and behavior of the client system, must be equally aware of the cultural determinants of their own behavior.

* Puerto Rican peasant.

61

Aside from general sensitivity to the problem of cross cultural influences, there appear to be some specific skills and knowledge areas that would be useful for social workers dealing with a Puerto Rican population in a New York City setting:

1. Ability to speak Spanish.

2. Knowledge of migration patterns.

3. Familiarity with the family patterns in the Puerto Rican community, including male/female relationships; respective family roles, responsibilities, duties and obligations; the nature of the extended family; child-rearing practices.

4. Familiarity with health care practices, including the use of non-professionals; the role of the spiritualist; the attitude toward the use of medical facilities.

5. Knowledge of leisure time activity preferences and the relationships of such preferences to other sociological roles.

6. Knowledge of religious practices and influence.

7. Particular Puerto Rican community patterns and institutions in New York City.

It is the belief of the writers that in order to incorporate in one's self the knowledge and sensitivity necessary to function effectively with the Puerto Rican population, the student is best prepared through an experience of total immersion. Such an experience was the objective of this project.

Footnotes:

1. From a Memorandum prepared by the Project Director for N.I.M.H., January 1972.

2. Puerto Rico Learning Center. Training Program, Fall Semester, 1973 for Hunter College School of Social Work. (Ponce, Puerto Rico, 1973).

3. Joseph Fitzpatrick. Puerto Rican Americans. (Englewood Cliffs, N.J.: Prentice-Hall, 1971).

4. Viktor Frankel. Man's Search for Meaning. (New York: Washington Square Press, 1963).

5. Fitzpatrick, op. cit.

CHAPTER 9

THE SETTING - PONCE

The second and third training cycles were conducted at the Puerto Rico
Learning Center in Ponce. Ponce (population 130,000) is the second largest city of
Puerto Rico, situated near the south coast of the island, a few miles from the ocean.

The project students arrived at San Juan International Airport, disembarked
from the large jetliner, and transferred to a girafa, one of the small propeller planes
accommodating about two dozen passengers which serve the island's major cities. (The
planes are nicknamed "the giraffes" because of their oddly shaped, long-necked fuselages.

The flight to Ponce takes about a half hour. Because the plane is so small,
it flies close to the ground, rather hugging the contour of the plains and mountains,
so that there is a good opportunity to observe the urban sprawl of the San Juan metropolitan area over the northern coastal plain, then the peculiar karst formations of the
foothills to the mountainous area which is dotted with farms and towns - and finally
the high mountain range from which the quick and steep descent to Ponce is made, to an
airport so diminutive in comparison with that of San Juan that one is immediately fore-
warned of the smallness of Ponce.

The newly arriving student would first be taken to the Puerto Rico Learning
Center, located in the center of town in a former convent - a quite charming compound
of buildings in typical Spanish colonial baroque style, with a cloister looking out
on a garden shaded by a huge tree. For many students, the convent would remain a haven
throughout their stay. They would get to know some of what travelers' guidebooks identify as major points of interest:

The Plaza Degetau - the main square with its shops, its rather undistinguished
cathedral and its garishly painted appendix, the Parque de Bombas (firehouse) in which
Ponenos seem to take a pride not easily understood by the outsider. The students would
learn in time about some of the social functions carried out in the Plaza. It is a
public park and community meeting place; near the Plaza one finds publicos (jitneys),
and with a little bit of luck and patience a taxi; it is the area where a single woman
walking alone late at night was signalling an offer of love for sale; it was the place
to go to learn how to become part of the distribution system for illicit drugs from
marijuana to heroin.

The city's two main industrial plants - a rum distillery and a cement factory
were little noted by our students. They had more to do with the local campus of the
University of Puerto Rico system and especially the Catholic University, where they attended lectures. Similarly, the local art museum was visited by quite a few students.
An attractive contemporary building housing a minor but interesting collection, it seems
to have served for some students as a comforting, familiar refuge from the strangeness
and stress of living in the barrio. Some of their accounts are reminiscent of the
feelings of many American visitors to Europe when they visit the museums of that continent. They can look, walk and sit down; if they are bored, at least they know they
are acquiring culture.

A refuge far more important than the museum was the Hotel Intercontinental,
perched in the hills above Ponce and reached by a narrow and somewhat perilously winding

road. It is the kind of place with which international hotel chains have dotted the globe. The architecture is in the modern international hotel style which easily is transplanted from continent to continent and tropical island to tropical island, and is given a local imitation authenticity by "native" decoration motifs so that the tourist may know which country he is visiting. Of course, the hotel has a swimming pool, a dancing bar and a shopping arcade. One is reminded of the remoteness and the provinciality of the place mainly by the fact that the gambling casino (a standard feature of Puerto Rican hotels designed for mainland tourists) looks like a somewhat rundown New York City poolroom, and that the main restaurant is transformed into an English-language movie house once or twice a week. But whatever the hotel's limitations, it was a haven to many of our students: there it was all right for them to behave as Americans (or as North Americans as they had learned to call themselves); there they were on their own territory even when dealing with Puerto Ricans, when asking for or accepting a dance, or when offering or accepting a drink.

This tourist's view of Ponce was changed abruptly once the student entered the real, day-to-day life of his host families and the barrios in which they lived. Ponce consists of about 30 barrios or neighborhoods, each with its distinctive characteristics. Some, especially those near the center of town, have streets lined with graceful columned houses, many of which are being restored to their original elegance. Others are a jumble of jerry-built frame buildings, some of them newly painted in cheerfully glossy blues, yellows and pinks. In the outlying areas, there are wooden shacks on stilts, with an intermixture of the concrete and cinderblock replacement housing sponsored by the local government. And finally, there are the urbanizaciones - lower to middle class housing developments: rows upon rows of detached and semi-detached homes on smallish plots, rather like some tropical version of the farther reaches of Queens, their depressing similarity slowly modified by the individual owners' more or less creative addition of porch enclosures in fancily wrought iron, gardens populated with colorful sculptures of dwarfs and mushrooms, and of course garages for the new car.

Our students got to know most of these barrios, not as mere picturesque relics of the past, not as mere slums about the existence of which they might get their social conscience exercised, and not as mere imitation-mainland suburbia, but rather as the real settings for the real lives of real people whose lives they shared and, to some extent, learned to understand during the following three months.

SECTION II

THE EXPERIENCE OF THE STUDENTS:
PROBLEMS AND REACTIONS

INTRODUCTION

The conflict between a new arrival's expectations and experience has been described by others as four stages. The first stage of fascination is followed by a second stage of hostility against the host culture, followed by a third stage of adjustment and a fourth stage of genuine biculturalism in which one is able to act in accord with host-culture norms. Having experienced culture shock in one culture does not prevent culture shock in the future, although it may provide the sojourner with some insights into why he feels as he does.[1] Through culture shock the visitor learns ways he is influenced by his own culture and specific ways other persons from other cultures are likewise influenced in their behavior.

The Cross-Cultural, Cross-Regional Drug Project, had as one of its major purposes the training of social workers to work with the Hispanic population of New York City.

The planning and organization of the project has already been discussed in earlier chapters. The words, reports, reactions, concerns and problems of the students themselves can provide the best insight into the nature of the project and the effect it had on the cultural values of the participants.

The nature of a cross-cultural experience implies a possible conflict between two cultures. This conflict involves the difference between expectations and experiences. The individual's expectation regarding a different culture is based on a limited amount of knowledge. The actual experience can be different from the expectation. This difference can be described as culture shock. Hall[2] defined culture shock as a "removal" or distortion of many of the familiar cues one encounters at home and the substitution for them of other cues which are strange. The term first introduced by Kalvero Oberg[3] describes anxiety resulting from losing one's sense of when to do what and how to do it - which seems to occur in stages. In the first incubation stage the visitor may feel genuinely euphoric about the exciting new culture around him. This is followed by a second stage of dealing with crises resulting from the "normal" daily activities which suddenly seem to present insurmountable difficulties generating hostility toward hosts for being "unreasonable". In the third stage, the visitor begins to understand the host culture and to regain his sense of humor. In the fourth stage, the visitor begins to accept the host culture in a balanced picture of positive and negative aspects. The fifth and final stage occurs when the visitor returns home and experiences reverse culture shock in his readjustment.

This section of the monograph is drawn from the material in the students' logs and in the reports which they were required to submit.

This section is divided into 4 major parts -- each of which represents an important part of their learning about the culture of Puerto Rico.

1. First Reactions

2. Living Arrangement

3. Communication and Language

4. The Family

    a) Extended Family
    b) Sex Roles
    c) Work Roles
    d) Family Roles
    e) Religion

The focus is on the students speaking, sometimes in a well organized academic fashion and sometimes in the manner of personal, individual expression. This is the story of what happened to a group of New York graduate social work students who wanted to learn to speak Spanish and to serve the Puerto Rican community more effectively. Unless otherwise noted, quotations in this section are from the students' logs and reports.

Footnotes:

1. R. J. Foster. Examples of Cross Cultural Problems Encountered by Americans Working Overseas: An Instructor's Handbook. (HUMRRO, 1965). As quoted by Paul Pederson, The Field and Focus of Cross Cultural Counselling, unpublished paper.

2. E. T. Hall. The Silent Language. (New York: Doubleday, 1959).

3. Kalvero Obert. "Cultural Shock and the Problem of Adjustment to New Cultural Environments." In D. Hoopes, Readings in Intercultural Communications. (Pittsburgh: University of Pittsburgh, 1972).

CHAPTER 10

FIRST REACTIONS

This chapter is to present the students' initial reactions to the barrio and to the families with which they were placed, and the coping devices they used to come to terms with the situation.

The First Week

The students arrived in Ponce on a Monday morning. They spent the first two nights at a guest house and the days at the Puerto Rico Learning Center, where they were offered a program of orientation to Puerto Rico and to barrio living.

> Taken to rooming house where we will spend the next two days before moving to the barrios. Group split in two, with 4 others and I in one place.

> First impressions: rooming house a disaster, rooms incredibly small. Ye god, if this is poverty may I never know the deprivation it inflicts upon its victims. I must stop comparing things to my middle class values. It must be very depressing for persons to live permanently in these types of surroundings.

Two days later, late Wednesday afternoon, their barrio trainer took them to the families with whom they were to live for the next 12 weeks.

The typical sequence of events when arriving at their new homes was to meet the family members present at that time, and to be shown their room and other accommodations. Shortly thereafter, they would be offered food - disconcerting experience for most of the students who were accustomed to the North American evening meal as a gathering of the family around the dinner table, and who suddenly were confronted with the custom of many lower social level Puerto Rican families of having each member of the family eat whenever he or she felt hungry.

> Yesterday I moved in with my family. ...My first night here the mother served me dinner - then served her husband and son. The same routine was followed tonight. She never eats with the family - in fact I never see her eat. The parents speak no English but the sons do. They are pretty good about helping me though and don't speak English too much around me. After dinner the family watches TV or talks. The boys to go school. I told Doña....I will wash the dishes as she prepares the food and I've followed this routine.

> Another student and I talked on the way home about routine and finding one's place in the home. It is what causes most of us the most discomfort - not knowing our "place".

Another stated:

> I am fascinated with all my circuits loaded. Several hours ago I moved into my new "home" and cannot organize my observations so I'll ramble. I sit in a bed covered by a much needed mosquito net with a

framed beer advertisment over my head and in a room filled with
someone else's belongings in addition to mine (I don't know why
these things are here or to whom they belong.) There is no fan,
no curtin, but the room has floor to ceiling walls (the guest house
didn't have it). If they have hot water I don't know about it.
My new "madre" is a black woman who looks to be about 60 who lives
with a white teenage boy. I'm uncertain about their relationship.
The madre has a store (small) downstairs which is open from 7 to
11 P.M. where she makes ham and cheese sandwiches for the neighborhood so that all seem to congregate here. There are stray, mangy
dogs all over who occasionally roam in the house and get literally
kicked out and screamed at. Playa de Ponce (Puerto Viejo), my
neighborhood, seems to be quite poor. My "madre" keeps lots of
birds, something like pigeons that fill the yard and whom she feeds.
She speaks no English. No one on the block so far speaks any English
and I don't understand the Spanish they speak either. (A local
dialect.) The words seem so slurred that they are unrecognizable to
me. The place isn't clean and there are a variety of insects including spiders. Most of what I see I can't interpret such as why all
the equipment in the house isn't lugged in and out. I was brought
to all the neighbors and in each house I would sit and they would ask
me questions and laugh. Perhaps as when a child learns to walk the
relatives are amused. Everything is incredibly strange.

Arrived at the L household and was greeted by Doña R., mother-in-
law. About an hour later, head of the household, Mr. L, arrived
and proceeded to call his friends and tell them that the Americana
was here. He also called his wife who arrived about a half hour
later. Shortly after her daughter and sister-in-law arrived.
Mrs. L made my supper and fed me before the other members of the
household and the meal time conversation was centered around myself.
When asked if the other members of the family would eat with me
she replied that they take meals by themselves whenever they wanted.
...materially I want for nothing but there is a prevailing physical
and emotional distance that is successfully maintained and helped
by my inability to speak the language.

Some housing arrangements did not work out and required change.

This was the day I moved into my second and now permanent Puerto
Rican home. I moved in and out of my first family in two days,
feeling quite uncomfortable with the limited space I was given and
the housing conditions in general, so I approached moving again with
considerable anxiety. Fortunately, it was abated as soon as I met
my new family and was offered accommodations suitable to me.

The R family has lived in an urbanización named Jardines del Caribe
since last December...(husband) drives into the city's center every
morning, affording us (Mrs. R and M) a lot of opportunity to speak...
The family is Methodist and they asked me my religion the first night.

Not only did the students have to make the transitions required to live with a new
family but they also had to learn to live in a new community with different manners,
ways, customs.

Came home by "público" for the first time. Learned the público tra-
vels specific route to town but returns by various other routes. Al-

most got lost. Can understand the feelings of anxiety a Puerto Rican in New York has the first time he encounters the vast subway system.

On the way home a man got in the bus, passed by me with a live chicken or I believe a rooster in a paper bag. The head sticking out of the bag. Took me a little by surprise. When we (students) all get off at my bus stop, I have rows of eyes watching us.

A few days after arrival, as part of the orientation program at the Puerto Rico Learning Center, each student was given a task to do.

We were each given a paper with directions on it; the purpose was to get us out into the streets of Ponce. At 12:00 I took my paper and clutching it in my hand, stepped outside of the gate of El Cuerpo de Paz. Before I stepped outside, I was very excited with my first adventure alone on a street in Ponce.

After I stepped outside I was gripped by genuine fear. I have never known this type of fear before! My paper instructs me to talk to someone in la Calle de Cristobal. I finally get up enough courage to ask a man the time. Literally flee after I do; I go into a drugstore. I choose the items I need. Decide to take a chance and to ask salesgirl in a chatty sort of way, if airmail costs 11¢ or 21¢. But she does not understand me. Over and over tries to explain to me that the envelopes cost 59¢. I feel stupid, embarrassed. This is really an ordeal. Gracias. senora! Leave. Walk for about one hour.

The paper says I must find someplace to eat. Meet H along the way. Purposely separate from her; this is too much of an adventure. It is something I must do by myself. Finally decide on a luncheonette type restaurant. I am impressed by how few luncheonettes there seem to be and wary, lest I enter someplace where women are not supposed to be. All Puerto Ricans in the restaurant; also I cannot read the signs. I walk out, afraid to sound stupid. I wander about. My first experience with Ponce heat. So hot! I feel faint. Realize I must find someplace soon or else, indeed, I will faint.

I finally enter a place with bar/restaurant outside and talk to the waitress. This is my first experience with the inquisitive Latin spirit. I must look a wreck. In vain try to tell this woman, who is looking at me inquisitively, what I want and finally give up with as much dignity as by that time I have left. I tell her I want the special of the day and what are habichuelas? (I certainly know now!) She orders my food, comes back, putters around my table, asks me some questions among which are "what's the matter, you don't have friends that you eat alone?" Finally takes it upon herself to go over word by word the written specials of the day. Makes me repeat after her. I feel much better. I now have a friend. She assures me that it is fine for me to come to this restaurant without a man (unaccompanied).

I feel much better after lunch. On the way back step in front of a car - driver to me "hey, Americana!" - just give him a wave of my hand - smile to myself as I get to the other side of the street. I am indeed a North American!

A new awareness of who one is, and how perceived by others.

Physical Adjustment

The new experience involved adaptation to physical conditions which sometimes were very unpleasant. The problems and the responses were many and varied.

The change of climate from New York to tropical Puerto Rico and the necessary physiological adaptation is not to be underestimated as a serious factor in early adjustment. The sounds of the "coqui" - tree frogs - at night, the noises of ubiquitous chickens and dogs into the night and early in the morning, the need for a mosquito net, the unaccustomed toileting arrangements all contribute to the feelings of strangeness. And, as one student noted "not having my own things" enhanced the malaise.

I haven't been bothered by the heat but my reaction has been one of exhaustion. I could stop at any moment of the day and take a siesta. I may end up sleeping away half of my time down here.

It is hard for me to be able to sift out many of my feelings now. When I finally snuggled under my mosquito net the noise of the birds, frogs and bugs outside was unreal...like something from an old movie.

Pervasive Exhaustion

Another factor that I have found difficult is that the workers here do not stop for a coffee break. During the sessions today I thought to myself "a cup of coffee would bring me back to life". One thing that was good today was that the rooms in J were air-conditioned. Otherwise I am sure I would have slept through a large part of the discussions. As it was, I almost fell asleep during the second discussion this morning. Early to bed at night hasn't helped so I guess I will just have to hope that the body will soon become adjusted.

Right now I feel exhausted. I got to bed at 10 P.M. which is about four hours earlier than I'm used to.

But I'm always a little tired especially in the evening. I think it's the strain of not having my own things, of being completely immersed in someplace strange. I feel like there is no way to get away.

Basta. More at another time. Only let me add that I try not to think about what I miss, or what I am not happy about. The minute that I do I'm lost - I'd get morose - my whole energy is living in the present day to day. Maybe after I understand and make my place I'll be able to plan.

The afternoon was spent at a meeting. It lasted for three hours and I really did not gain much from the discussion because I think I had used up all my ability in the morning. I was embarrassed later to realize that I had slept through part of it. I can't seem to find a way to counteract fatigue.

Well that's all I can do for now - I'm extremely tired, I have a terrible cold and today I felt like passing out twice probably a combination of the 1) weather - rainy, just about every day, humid, extremely hot; 2) the beach - too much sun last weekend; 3) the chickens and the dogs keep me up until about 1:00 a.m., and then wake me up at about 5:15 a.m.

Let me just note this so that there is no misunderstanding - I like it here very, very much. My "parents", "brothers", and "sisters" are beautiful, warm and very simpatico, I merely want you to be aware of the living conditions - to say the least it's not like being in New York. (The chickens and dogs are outside of the house, of course!)

Interpersonal and Adjustment Problems

The initial period of excitement, uncertainty and anxiety was followed by a let-down as individuals faced their real ties and struggled to cope with their new circumstances.

Spanish lessons going well. Had a culture simulation session. Instructor at the Learning Center very unsympathetic and unable to empathize with groups' housing and adjustment problems.

The schedule was arduous.

Today I had a sudden glimpse into the impossibility of our task here in Ponce. Ex. my average day:

Get up at 6:00. At center by 9:30. 1/2 hour to talk, have coffee, write. 8-12 - usually Spanish, with 1/2 hour break.
12:00 - 1:30 - lunch
1:30 - 5:30 - Spanish and cross-cultural lectures/discussions
From 6:30 then to 10:30-11:00 (by this time I am usually very sleepy) I have to:

- spend an hour or two with my family (the only time of the day I have with them - I constantly have in mind that I should spend more time with them, even if I don't feel like it - 1) to be gracious; 2) because it is part of my so-called cross-cultural training; and 3) because I must gain their trust so that I can write a research paper about them and thereby graduate.)
- study Spanish
- write letters and do the work to send to New York
- read (which I hardly ever do)
- bathe etc.
- eat dinner, help with the dishes.

This then is a 10-15 hour a day "job". I am going to have to establish some priorities or else I will become very frustrated. I already feel a bit overwhelmed.

The tensions and discomfort caused by all the new adaptations required by the new academic program and the "barrio living" brought forth a wave of complaints.

Group conferences could have been more productive if group members didn't use them to constantly ventilate their dissatisfactions. The negative things about the program got emphasized while not sufficient time was given to elaborate upon the positive and meaningful aspects of this program.

This week has been a trying one. I suppose a lot of the pressures of being here hit me, but I felt defensive, nervous, a bit out of it. (Faculty member) came down from New York City and it was good to see her, but I sometimes feel that what has been said somehow gets changed around. She was very patient in listening to our feedback, which at some points was quite heated. At least we felt afterward we had straightened some things out.

Wednesday we met in (faculty member's) room. Things got a bit heavy, and we dumped quite a bit on (faculty member) not all of which was warranted. We also dumped quite a bit on each other. It finally settled down when the P.R. social worker (who had been an exchange student at Hunter) came and spoke to us.

During this week I must admit that I began to see things happening in the group that disturbs me. The cohesiveness is beginning to crumble. Members are less mindful of the feelings of their colleagues. There is a sharpness creeping into the atmosphere. Complaining is becoming a habit, rather than a necessity. I'm withdrawing from the group more. I don't enjoy gripe sessions at my age. If there is a legitimate complaint it should be surfaced, discussed and dispensed with. Constant griping can sour any experience.

My main feeling today is that I am so tired of rehashing the events of the first weeks with (faculty member). It is for this reason I separate from the group at the hotel and go down to dance. What fun!

I have become increasingly impatient with the group in the last week. Part of this is my new friendships, part of it is that I do not enjoy rehashing unhappy details. I am not homesick, nor am I depressed and I'm quite sure that I want to be right where I am now. In large measure this is an experiment to help me understand how much of New York I really need and how much I can leave behind. It is not an easy experiment by any means but it is one I feel I must do right now.

I wish I had more empathy with those members of the group who really are suffering and I do to a certain extent - but my lack of suffering in these beginning weeks is not permitting the closeness that would come with common suffering. I do know that I feel very separate from the group at this point.

After living with their families for some time, one student commented:

Some students are expressing negative feelings about the family-barrio living experience. I personally think that much of the feeling reflects a lack of awareness about what it means to live in another environment. It reflects a feeling of being alone and not having control over the environment.

What are the causes for these feelings? Some are expected in this type of experience especially from a group of people used to being very independent and free of family obligations.

In this second stage of adjustment, when the students are confronted with seemingly insurmountable difficulties, hostility toward the program and host culture is to be expected. Some of the criticism of the program design, after several weeks of participation were appropriate and realistic. Many of the students had moved beyond complaint and frustration to the stage of beginning to cope and adapt.

We have been stuck into a program (designed) for Peace Corps volunteers with little or no adjustment made for our special situation and goals. For example, of the 11 people here, 6 have lived outside of the United States for a year or more. Everyone of the rest has traveled quite a bit in Europe. This adds up to considerable experience yet we have been treated as though we have just left Ohio for the first time. We have had 25 hours of cross-cultural training so far. I feel very strongly that there is a rich lode of experience to be mined from living here but am beginning to despair of getting any help in reaching it.

Comfort Bits

Being faced with a strange setting, where one's usual forms of behavior do not evoke the expected responses creates within individuals a sense of tension. Different ways of coping with the sense of confusion or loss of unfamiliarity become "comfort bits". For the Norte Americano, Coca-Cola and a visit from welcoming "fellow Americans" become some of those "comfort bits".

> Back at our boarding house, we sit on the veranda and N got rum, I got cokes, two of the Peace Corps people came over, C and T - I really appreciated that they came over, and our group gave each other support as tomorrow we will meet our families.

Despite the maturity of the students, careful selection and preparation, each of the students faced the move to the barrios and living with a family with anxiety of varying degrees. Most of the students had left their families of origin for some time, and developed their own life styles. Many had given up family living by the time they graduated from college and maintained their own apartments, and arranged their living to their choice. For some, an opportunity to escape from the "strange" barrio and family was important. The only cosmopolitan hotel in town provided the opportunity for a "refuge".

> Some of us (North American students) go up to the Intercontinental Hotel after school. Feels almost like a refuge.

Some other students resented the group members who needed this escape and refused to join.

> The group is going to the bar at the Intercontinental Hotel for drinks. I refuse to carry my New York lifestyle here. If I'm to assimilate I must live more or less similarly to the customs of the people, for me being a participant observer is participating.

Over and over again students refer to relaxing and speaking English together.

> The struggle to communicate in an unfamiliar language appears to produce a pervasive tension.

> On a visit with the other New York students we had a very relaxing time. I began to realize how important speaking English was to really relaxing.

The weekends provided some opportunity for members of the group to share more familiar patterns with people who had the same frame of reference in terms of past experience and language.

> In the breaks in the Latin band at the dance, we played the only North American music in the jukebox, some Carole King records.

> I also think about Puerto Ricans being in a new environment and
> wanting to do the same thing - listen to their own music. What we
> were told in one of the early sessions, certainly is true, re: com-
> fort bits, the name given to those things one actually misses when
> one is transplanted into another culture. I miss privacy, quiet, old
> movies (but not television), my cat, and, of course, my friends, and
> my books. I miss my family.

In this instance, the student was describing a weekend where several of them "escaped"
to a resort area together and were at a bar where all the music in the jukebox was
Puerto Rican - with the exception of one Continental favorite, which became unexpect-
edly popular with the New York group in their nostalgia.

> An on another weekend:

> At Boqueron (a resort), swam, slept, talked, ate dinner and watched
> the Mets lose the World Series (something else I would not pay any
> attention to if I was in New York). Here it assumed some importance.

> Not too keen on returning to Ponce, although I really like my "family"
> and am treated well.

In this quote we see the ambivalence toward the experience and the yearning for the
familiar, i.e., the World Series.

> Saturday - went to Boquerin Beach with rest of group of students.
> Ate some real food for a change.

The familiar is the "real" food as contrasted with the Puerto Rican diet. Eating the
traditional diet with families produced its share of discomfort. Fear of offending
and sheer hunger caused the students to eat the heavily starched diet and a variety
of items some would have preferred to avoid.

Feeling Like Strangers

All students experienced a good deal of anxiety at the prospect of having
to share the life of an as yet unknown family, in an alien culture, speaking a language of which but few of them had even a working knowledge. One student, as her plane
flew over the city of Ponce in its landing approach, found herself "looking down at all
the houses, hoping for some 'sign' to show me which one was going to be my house".
A feeling of anxiety was expressed by all the students in their logs or in personal
communications to project staff members and fellow students.

Our students were strangers to their new families, and felt the most acute
sense of alienation at the time of their initial encounter with the family. All of
them felt that they were being observed or tested, which was, of course, true. They
were unsure about their place in the family, and the customs or rules they should
honor. Some of their initial reactions are noted here.

Coping Devices

The newcomer to any group is, of course, a stranger. Some people feel comfortable in this role, either because they are less aware of others, or because they
are secure enough in their own sense of self to accept and perhaps even enjoy the
novelty of the situation. For some students, discomfort was clearly the cominant
reaction. All keenly felt that they were being observed and tested.

During the first mealtime, I was the focus of attention for the whole family.

I'm sure they are comparing me to (a previous PRLC boarder) in addition to testing me in other ways. ...At this point I believe that I am still the center of observation and testing.

A wide range of coping mechanisms was used to deal with the problem of being a stranger. These mechanisms were determined by a variety of factors. Some of them had to do with the objective conditions they encountered, the reception offered by the family, the housing conditions, and so on. Other factors were more subjective, such as the ability to use the Spanish language. Or they might be the special complex set of coping responses developed by each individual to novel and anxiety-producing situations, ranging all the way from helpless crying to a "take-charge" stance.

Here are some of the coping devices as they are described by the students.

Helplessness and mobilization of anger

> My room has no door - just a curtain. The daughter's room is adjacent to mine and to get to her room, you have to walk through mine. Also, there's no bathroom inside the house, just a really gross outhouse that I can't see myself going near let alone using...I'm not sure if I should laugh or cry. ...When I brought my suitcase to my room, I thought I'd at least be able to have a good cry...

This student, after her initial reaction of helplessness, mobilized her anger and demanded to be transferred to another family. The transfer was arranged by the Puerto Rico Learning Center.

Trying to find security by turning to student group.

Most students found the Hunter group at the Puerto Rico Learning Center a source of security and comfort at various times during their stay in Ponce. At least one of them used this coping device even before meeting her family:

> Later on when R (Puerto Rico Learning Center staff member) comes around to tell me where I will live, I become surprisingly tense. Carefully dot on a map of Ponce which we have been given where the others will be. Makes me feel more secure. Had not expected to be so nervous about tomorrow's move as I feel now.

Counteraction: Becoming part of the family.

Many students handled their anxiety by quickly identifying with the family, as the Barrio Live-in Program had instructed them to do. One student reports:

> (The third day after meeting the family) I went shopping with the family to a supermercado. ...I want to feel that I'm not just an observer but a participant. I really feel like a member of the family as I am included in everything - so pushed the cart.

Counteraction: The "take-charge" stance

At least one student who felt quite free to acknowledge her anxiety as she anticipated her new surroundings coped with it by assuming a "take-charge" stance which she maintained throughout her stay with the family. Here it was the student who was the mothering, helping person; one might say that she was a live-in social worker. This attitude comes through in her very first reaction:

> My lady (mother) is extremely nice, friendly, helpful without being overbearing - she continues to try to make me feel comfortable and welcome and seems to need feedback in this area. She may also need some companionship since her husband is away so often.

Not knowing one's place - and asking for rules.

When one finds oneself in a strange environment, the customs and rules of which are unknown, the simplest coping device is to ask what the rules are. One woman student described this process:

> (another student) and I talked on the way home about routine and finding one's place in the home. It is what causes each of us the most discomfort - not knowing our "place". ...I had to go to get cigarettes (at night) and I asked if that was O.K. I'm not sure if B (a male family member) accompanied me for company or because women are suppose to have someone with them after dark.

As this example shows, asking for rules may not result in clear instructions. Apparently, the student was told that it was appropriate to go out for an errand after dark, but she was not sure whether it was appropriate for a woman to go out alone after dark.

> It's difficult to have to ask for everything. For example late this evening I wanted some juice or anything. I never know if I'm doing something that might offend them. Also, everything smells so different, I can't even tell who or what smells like what. Also the toilet is never flushed and I don't know how they feel about my flushing it. Maybe there is a water shortage, maybe it's a custom, maybe it's idiosyncratic.

Not knowing one's place - and feeling one's way.

Another way of coping with an alien culture is to feel one's way in rather than to ask directly for a rule of behavior. This technique was used often, perhaps most frequently in the context of mealtime behavior. For most students, the eating customs of their host families were alien, and since the friendly, solicitous, or matter-of-fact offer of food was one of the first actions they had to deal with, they had to invent reactions on the spot. Some felt their way in by trying to make sure they were not violating the rules.

One student reports:

> The mother asked me when I wanted to eat - this is about one half hour after I arrived. I explained that I wanted

to eat when they ate. "Mama" told me that they all eat when
they are hungry. After some further discussion - when I was
sure she wasn't just being super-polite and this was the way
it was - I accepted.

Others felt their way by equivocating so as to avoid possible conflict: "My 'mother'
asked me if I pray before eating. I said only on holidays or _fiestas_."

Not knowing one's place - and making one's place.

Finally, one way of coping with the insecurity about one's place in a new
group is to make one's place. This coping device, when applied with appropriate sensitivity, usually creates a kind of stability and security both for the newcomer and the
group he has joined. Here is how one student used this technique:

I've started with my dishwashing routine (washing dishes
for the whole family while her "mother" prepared food,
thus keeping her company in the kitchen even though she
cannot talk to the "mother" due to her limited command of
the Spanish language). Also decided I'd better have some
study routine so I explained that I had lessons and would
study for an hour in my room.

This student made her place with the new group both by becoming part of it
(the dishwashing routine) and by marking off boundaries of privacy (the study routine).

Language, Communication

The initial reaction of a newcomer to a group is, of course, determined to
a large extent by the ability to communicate with the group. We have noted above a
variety of coping devices. All of them depended to some degree on the most important
medium of communication: language. Few of our students, at the time they met their
families, had a working knowledge of the Spanish language. Of course, this influenced
their reactions. Two extreme examples: first, a student who spoke almost no Spanish:

No one on the block so far speaks any English and I don't understand the Spanish they speak either. For example when (mother) calls
V. it sounds to me like "Alo". The words seem so slurred that they
are unrecognizable to me... Everything is incredibly strange.

Contrast this with the relaxed description of a student fluent in Spanish:

Doña R spoke to the man who brought me from the Learning Center
about payment, laundry, etc. Turning to me, she declared the house
was mine while I stayed there... Through conversing, I learned
(Doña R's life history.)

Adjustment Process

And then, following Oberg's stages, in the third stage the newcomer begins
to understand the host's culture, balances positives and negatives and regains his
sense of humor, as demonstrated by these short comments.

Meanwhile I'm not pushing anything - I find I am re-evaluating
goals on a daily basis, if I don't get too much out of a group in
terms of learning about addicition, I'm learning more Spanish - so

it goes.

I'm observing more of my physical surroundings and am beginning to enjoy my stay here in terms of having good experiences.

CHAPTER 11

LIVING ARRANGEMENTS

Barrio housing provided the students, varied considerably. It included in lower middle class "urbanizaciones", housing developments of neat one story family homes, public housing apartment dwellings, "caserios", old and new housing of varied descriptions.

On a faculty visit to a household in Ponce, to which one of the students was assigned, we entered a room, one flight up, over a shop, in semi-darkness. It was mid-day with the sun shining brightly, but the shutters were closed to keep the sun out and the house cool. The building, of wood on a cement block base, looked dilapidated and poorly kept. In the living room, the main source of light was the ubiquitous TV screen, from what could be seen, the large room was cluttered with an assortment of chairs, a sofa, and other pieces of furniture - not clearly distinquishable in the dim light. A small porch faced the street in front of the living room, and all other rooms were in back of the living room. The householders were friendly and solicitous. Perhaps because of the semi-darkness and the appearance of the outside of the building, the interior, too, seemed dingy and oppressive.

Another faculty visit was to Playa de Ponce, an old section of the City which includes the waterfront and is generally described as a major slum of Ponce. The house stood on pilings about 9 or 10 feet off the ground and was reached by two stairways located roughly at opposite ends of the building; there was a side entrance (the formal entrance) and the back entrance. The space under the building was used for storage and was inhabited by a number of chickens. I was told later that "mama" operated a small store - tienda - at the back where she sold some food items to boys at a nearby school.

The front room had just been finished in a dark plywood, by the father of the household. The center of the room was largely filled by a permanent bar (recently constructed) from which the family members now seemed to take their meals. The room had the look of the interior of some of the small bars and restaurants in Ponce. Other furniture included several wooden chairs, a small table and a low coffee table. The other rooms (kitchen, bath, bedrooms), ran off a central hall. The house was not close to others and the plot had space on either side. The living room was bright and cheerful on this sunny day. The TV set was on prominent display.

In contrast, the building in which another student lived, a few blocks away, in the same barrio (Playa de Ponce), was a dingy looking, unpainted old wooden one story house (traditional Poncean facade) in a closely crowded group of homes with only a few feet of space on either side.

A male student lived with a family in an apartment, one flight up over a store, on a busy street in the downtown section of Ponce, a few blocks from the city's main square. The building was one of closely packed series which ran along both sides of a heavily trafficked street. A porch faced the street from which family members often viewed events below. Furnishings in the front room were sparse but neatly maintained. The rooms did not seem to be cluttered and gave the impression of order and organization. This was an "old style" wooden building, the rooms with high ceilings, a feature of older (pre-air conditioned) tropical housing.

Two urbanizaciones where students were housed, were also visited. Both neighborhoods were neat and well kept, with rows of cement, one story, one family homes, each with a garden and evidence of proprietory interest.

Privacy

Privacy, so highly valued by our young adult North American students, was not easy to achieve in barrio living. By agreement with each family, each student was to have private sleeping quarters in their barrio home. One student observed:

> It is interesting to note that there is no word for "privacy" in Spanish. It is probably here that the two cultures clash the most. Students and volunteers have a hard time with the lack of privacy.

Another reported:

> It is very hard to study or write due to lack of privacy. It appears that very little activity is done alone. Bedroom doors are never closed. There is constant talking.

The reference to a lack of privacy, to nothing being done alone, and the constant group activity in households was repeated by most of the students, as indicated by the following brief comments.

> So many people come in and out all nite long (aunts, grandmothers, cousins, neighbors) that they could spend the entire time in greetings and salutations.

> Everything is done "together" in the house, including when I get washed in the bathroom, change my clothes, and write this log. All the boys are curious to know what I am doing. They ask me to explain what I am writing, to explain what a nail clipper is used for, and what is carbon paper. A was dancing in my room.

> I get tired some times because everything is done en masse, and has all the confusion and inconvenience of large groups. Everything gets done but in what appears to be a fairly disorganized way. For instance we may decide to go shopping right away which ends up being an hour or so later.

> Unlike other group members, I do not miss New York - only the privacy of my apartment.

Some of the arrangements were quite primitive.

> Oh yes, there's an outhouse here and I must take care of the morning necessities, i.e., washing and brushing teeth, etc., by walking outside and around the back into a little shack-like hut where I wash; another where I urinate and still another where I shower.

On the family moving to new quarters one of our young women recounted her horror:

> I had a few minutes of panic when I realized the family planned for me to share a bedroom with Doña C (the mother). I thought they were just joking until I asked where my bed was. When I heard I just walked out front and wondered how the hell I would

survive in such a situation. I explained to my "cousins" and they
were supportive, so armed with dictionary, I went to see Doña C .
Of all that I said she fastened on my need to study as a reason to
have my own room.

Mealtime

It became evident that the expectation that families ate together was a cultural norm of middle class North Americans and mealtime was an early adaptation for
each student. A typical observation was:

> People ate in rotation. I was generally first. For the most part
> the boys ate first, then the girls, though it seemed to depend on
> when each arrived home from work or school. The father usually
> ate last since he was usually the last to arrive home. (Father
> worked almost everyday including Sunday.)

From the very first day, expectations for behavior were not as anticipated.

> (dinner time, first day)
> I was asked if I was hungry and of course I said yes - I thought
> both M and A were waiting for me before eating. However, this was
> not the case. I ate first and later on in the evening A ate (his
> wife fixed his plate). I don't remember seeing his wife eat at all.
> A, Sr. mentioned that his wife usually eats a heavy meal during lunch.

The group quickly learned that the basic staples of the Puerto Ricans were rice and
beans.

> Tonight I ate alone again. I had my usual rice, beans, beer, pine-
> apple juice (for a change) and avocados. "Mama" seemed very conscious
> of the fact that my meals are not varied (understatement of the
> year) because she said (en espanol, of course) that I have rice and
> beans again. Food was served by mama in separate plates and I put
> it into the plate and ate with my one fork. Brother R did sit down
> at table with same food after a while, on one plate - quietly ate and
> then brought empty plate back into kitchen. After I finished meal I
> brought my plate back into kitchen and put it into a rather small sink.

> Note: family really does not eat together, as far as I've been able
>   to observe. I've never seen "mama" or for that matter "papa"
>   eat a single thing. I have seen "papa" drink beer, but nothing
>   else. I don't know where L (daughter) eats, however, I suspect
>   that she eats here. At night, after returning from church, she
>   usually watches TV here with "mama" until 11:30 p.m.

Dinner - When I arrived home from the Learning Center the family had
already eaten. M and C were finishing their rice in the living room
as they were watching TV. I had rice and beans with ground chicken.
The mother served me water and gave me a paper towel to use as a nap-
kin. I finished the meal alone and began to talk with the mother on
the balcony.

Over and over again, the theme that families do not eat together is repeated.

> I got home at about 6 p.m. and we ate right-away. This time all of
> us sat down together to eat except for son who was going out to a

meeting. The rest of us, myself, the other son, the daughter, the mother, the father and his father sat down at the same time. We ate fried chicken, salad (lettuce and tomato) and rice and beans. Water was served but no milk. Later the mother asked me if I wanted milk. No one else drinking, I didn't either.

While the host families were generous, there was a feeling that some families deprived themselves in order to be hospitable.

First day at my new home. I first met my new "father", "mother" and two sons named J and L, after I had an initial discussion with the father, showed me around the house. I learned that the father built the house - he's a carpenter. The mother asked me when I wanted to eat - this was about 1/2 hour after I arrived - I explained that I wanted to eat when they ate. "Mama" told me that they all eat when they're hungry. After some further discussion - when I was sure she just wasn't being super-polite and this was the way it was - I accepted.

The mama gave me rice, beans and lamb chops. All foods were in a separate plate. I was given a fork and a plate. "Mama" told me to put rice, beans and lamb chops in same plate. Oh yes, she gave me avocadoes. I ate on a table that's situated in the same room with TV, radio (stereo), couch, two chairs and entrance to "papa" and sister's rooms. The dining table is approximately 15 ft. from door. R and G did sit down at table with me after a little while and they ate the same. I asked for a knife...

From what I could gather from past observations and from what R tells me, there is no regular mealtime - the children eat as they please. R told me that his mother saves the meat for G and me. T buys meat but I've not seen it for three days now, tonight I ate bean soup, bread and vegetables.

The children eat lots of junk - pie, ice cream, bread and mayonnaise, American cheese, dry cereal, Koolaid, y arroz y habichuelas.

A little after 6 p.m., the mother came in to tell me that dinner was ready. There were 4 places set. Three for her children and one for me. We ate asopao (with rice and meat), mashed potatoes and salad. I believe the salad was for my sake as nobody else touched it. There are two sons and one daughter, two sat down with me at the table but the younger son ate later as he was out on the porch involved in a game. The mother did not pressure him to come in and eat. When the other son got up, the mother sat down to eat. We did not wait for the father.

The group learned the expected standards of "sanitation" are not necessarily the same as they were used to:

Mama ate half a banana and then put it on my plate - I ate it. This morning L did not want all of his eggs so she added his leftover to L (a boarder) eggs - still in the pan.

The students found themselves eating new unfamiliar foods - not always because they wanted to, but because they did not want to insult the hosts:

The mother here walked through from the kitchen with two dead
doves. I started, and she calmly went to the side yard and
plucked them. She then proceeded to tell me that she preferred
fried dove to fried chicken! and they also made great soup! So
it looks like I'll be eating dove. Seems symbolic or ironic or
something. And with J (another student) eating the rooster she
helped to kill, and R (also a student) eating goat, we're all
sampling gamut.

Apparently some students were not able to put their individual preferences
aside in order to be the "good guest".

P, smiling, said I do not respect his mother because I do not
like the beans she prepared. He said that I don't like his
mother's cooking. She was at the table when he spoke. Her
face appeared to have no reaction to what he said. She did not
say anything. I said that I like her cooking but that I don't
like beans. The mother said that it is hard for her to buy beef
steak. She said she received $562 per month from the government
to pay her expenses. That includes food, housing, transportation
and two visits to the doctor per week. She said she is only able
to buy clothes when she has a Learning Center volunteer live in
her house. I asked her for some more rice. She said K did not
eat yet. She asked me if I wanted some of her meal. I said no
thank you. She is an unbelievable woman; she sacrifices much for
her children and she allows time out for my welfare. She tells
me what barrios are dangerous to walk in and where to buy things,
at a reasonable cost, etc.

This student did learn that it was embarrassing and disturbing to the family when their
offerings were rejected. It was not the expected behavior.

There are not special eating arrangements. Who eats at the table
depends on who happens to be home and ready to dine. There are
times when two persons share one chair. When all family members
are home such as Saturday and Sunday, some dine in the kitchen and
others in the living room. It is not unusual for close friends and
extended family members to eat with the family without previous or
advanced notice of any kind. If it happens to be dinner time, the
offer to participate in the evening meal is extended to all persons
then within the home, including visitors.

The joy of sharing is displayed in many forms within this very poor
household.

The students, too, began to contribute special treats for the household.

I am beginning to feel at home. I bought Coca Cola for the family
as a treat. Family hasn't got money for any basic luxuries such
as sodas and soft drinks.

Stopped in market, bought groceries. The family was happy to see me.
The brothers were very warm as usual.

CHAPTER 12

COMMUNICATION AND LANGUAGE

Puerto Ricans in New York City

We have already referred to some of the language problems which many Puerto
Ricans encounter as they come to New York and find themselves immersed in an alien
environment where even the simplest everyday communication may become a serious and
sometimes quite frightening problem. The current pressures toward making New York a
bilingual city at many levels, especially in the schools, may affect the young and
upwardly mobile in time. But the old who have remained physically and psychologically
tied to their barrio still have to cope with the cold fact that many people whose advice
they need simply do not speak their language.

In social work practice, this often means that Puerto Ricans applying for
social services cannot explain what they need at the most elementary level of verbal
communication. Tendler (1965)[1] and Garcia (1971)[2] have examined some of the resulting
problems. Perhaps we can best illustrate this by the example reported by one of the
students whose interest in the project was stimulated by the following experience:

> The student who was placed in a large city hospital came to a
> member of the project staff requesting information about the pro-
> ject because she felt a desperate need for Spanish language compe-
> tence and cultural understanding. She had been taking Spanish les-
> sons for several summers on her own but still had only a minimum
> skill, and she was impressed with the fluency of the students who
> had spent the previous semester in Puerto Rico. The faculty member
> asked her to describe situations where a knowledge of Spanish might
> have helped. The student answered that there were many, and then pro-
> ceeded to describe an incident that had taken place recently.

> The student happened to be downstairs at the main social service
> desk when a very upset woman, accompanied by a 12 year-old child,
> came in. The child, frightened, said he couldn't speak English and the
> woman only spoke Spanish. The secretary in the social service office
> responded by getting angry because the woman could not explain what
> she wanted. The student was anxious to get on with her work, but felt
> she had to rescue the woman who could only explain that there was some-
> thing wrong with the child. The secretary insisted that she could not
> get in touch with the pediatrics department unless she knew what the
> problem was. Fortunately for the woman, the student was there and
> finally able to connect the woman with the service she needed. One
> wonders what happens to all the others for whom a Spanish-speaking
> worker, even one with limited competence, is not available.

In this instance, the child was ostensibly to be the translator. The use of translators
has severe limitations. Frequently a child is kept out of school to serve as a translator. Some of the content and meaning gets edited either because the client does not want
the translator to know, or because the translator may change the interpretation. In the
Hispanic context, the value of respeto (respect) comes in as an often critical variable.
Dependence on a younger person, especially one's own child, is a violation of that value
concept. The violation becomes even more serious when the older person is a male, and

86

most serious when he is the father.

Our Language Programs

The basic idea of our successive language programs was simple enough. Puerto Rican clients had difficulty communicating their needs to workers at the most elementary level. The workers not only knew little about Puerto Rico or Puerto Ricans and their culture, but did not speak even a little Spanish. It seemed sensible to develop a program which would at least make the workers meet the clients half-way; the workers should have some knowledge of the language and, in battling their own difficulties with el idioma, increase their understanding of some of the clients' difficulties, hesitancies and resentments.

As others may wish to develop programs with similar goals, it may be worth recounting briefly the sequence of approaches we have taken.

In preparation for the first training cycle, an introductory language course was offered to all students enrolled in the school at that time. The course was designed to respond to the entreaties of many social work students to acquire at least the rudiments of the language, and also to recruit candidates for the Project.[3] The course was attended by two of the present authors, and evaluated as being of clearly superior quality. However, it attracted only a limited number of students. Attendance was desultory, and student performance mediocre. The fact that the course was offered from 6 to 8 in the evening and without credit may have had something to do with this.

The students selected for the first cycle took an additional intensive six-week summer language course,[4] for 2-1/2 hours each morning. Attendance was required and monitored by faculty.

It was hoped that this linguistic preparation would enable the students to audit the courses and field observations in the institution with which the project was associated during the first cycle. This was not the case. One student's experiential report summarizes as well as anything else, the difficulties of this cycle, particularly at the beginning.

> Although I had prepared myself for the worst, I don't think I really had expected to be thrown into a situation during the first week where Spanish would be the language of all the lectures, and the situation was overwhelming.

> The language problem, in addition to living and traveling difficulties has left me with an emotional experience that has drained my psychic and physical energy, leaving me little to concentrate on the continued need to overcome the need for proficiency in the language.

> I understood next to nothing in the observation through a one-way mirror of group discussions by patients, and very little of the discussion by the professional personnel. The verbal exchange was very rapid. To be honest - had it been slower it would have made little difference.

As a result of the experiences in the first cycle, the 2nd and 3rd cycles were relocated to the Puerto Rico Learning Center. The program there consisted of intensive language training in small classes, and of living with a local family where usually only Spanish was spoken, as well as cognitive cultural content provided by faculty of Catholic University of Ponce.

The language program was designed to provide each student with sufficient expertise to communicate in Spanish at a basic level with social agency personnel and clients. The language training was related to social welfare and drug programs A special bibliography was developed. Each student was regularly given some feedback by his language instructor covering his progress in the class. The classes generally included no more than five people.

The Foreign Service Institute language test was administered at the beginning, in the middle and at the end of the training period, to measure the progress of the group. Classes were conducted conversationally and students used their living experiences as the content for the class. One student indicated in her log:

> Today I gave a speech for seven minutes in my Spanish class on the identity crisis of the Puerto Rican both here and in New York. Each of us had to talk on one aspect of what we had discussed in our lecture at Catholic University yesterday. I was really surprised I did it! And fairly well, too, after only four weeks.

Stages of Language Development

In this Chapter, our interest is focused on the student experiences resulting from the total immersion process as they relate to the ability to communicate verbally. From the students' reports, we identified five major stages of development of linguistic competence: 1) disorientation; 2) barrio living as a motivator and reinforcer; 3) ongoing strain of alienation; 4) attempts to try out one's competence; 5) understanding of linguistic variation.

1) Disorientation

Student reports on their initial disorientation abound. They found themselves placed in an environment where they lacked even the simplest ways of communicating verbally. They were made sharply aware of this by the "go-to" task which was one of the first assignments given them by the Learning Center. Here are two examples:

> We were each given a slip of paper with individual instructions to follow and two hours in which to do it. Mine read, "walk straight from Calle Isabella Gate to take a look at the outside building of Carcel Municipal de Ponce, once there pray you'll never be inside for the rest of your life, walk around Calle Castillo to see the old houses, etc. Walk inside the Plaza del Mercado, try to talk to people asking for the prices of food, have lunch there and come back to the Center." So, o.k., I finally figured out that Carcel was the jail and to my surprise I found out that nobody stopped me when I walked right up to the gate. Down Calle Castillo where many lawyers and architects had offices, and where there was a house with a distinct Georgian flavor. My favorite was the Plaza del Mercado. It was just like the marketa on 110th Street, only with more livestock. I finally got to asking what things were. It was fascinating and at the same time incredibly motivating to learn Spanish.

Another student reported:

> We had an assignment today to go along to different parts of the city for two hours and come back and talk about it. My piece of paper just said to take the público and go to Central Street. I, of course, thought that Central Street would be the "central street". My first público ride went o.k. I couldn't quite figure out whether it was best to pay in the beginning, in the end, or if it mattered. I was struck

by how many people they crowded into one car in the back seat. Then
The driver let me out on a street which was much narrower than I expected.

Out in some place where I had no idea where I was. No stores, only
houses, roosters and trees. I walked down the street a ways and found
a few stores but they really didn't fit my conception of stores. No
signs outside advertising what they were selling as far as I could tell.
I went in and requested a pack of Salem cigarettes and they couldn't
understand me. Later I discovered that they pronounced "Salem" differently because of the vowel sounds. I asked the storekeeper where I
was, which understandably he found a strange question. I was in barrio
Baldarioty.

I had totally lost any sense of east, west, etc. There didn't seem to
be too many people around. I passed two schools and felt very strange
walking by myself down those streets, not feeling like I could understand anything I was seeing. I asked a few people the names of the
schools and really didn't understand the answers, but smiled anyway.
I wasn't quite sure about how to get back, but I heard a horn honking,
and sure enough it was a público driver, much to my relief. I was
struck by the poverty, heat and the lack of familiarity. I felt timid
and frightened.

2) Barrio Living

Living with a family where Spanish was the only language spoken proved to be
one of the strongest motivators and reinforcers for learning the language. The relatively exotic situation of the first day's "go-to" task might have been an adventure,
none too different in structure from that of the traveler who finds himself stranded
outside of the tourist circuit catering to the English-speaking trade. But now the
student was faced with ongoing problems of day-to-day communication. This ranged from
simple things such as the word for "fork" or "plate" to often complex interactions in
which feelings or attitudes toward family had to be expressed - and just to make the
task that much more difficult, had to be expressed in a culturally acceptable manner.
Obviously this was not just a matter of what the student did or did not do. What the
family members did or did not do was equally important. The variety of transactional
systems were very different from family to family. In some instances the system was
simplified and formalized in such a way that the student was simply treated as (and
perceived himself as) a boarder. This in turn simplified the linguistic transactions,
as they would then be mostly confined to the practicalities of the living arrangements.
More frequently, complex relationships with mutual emotional investments were made.
The convention at the Learning Center of referring to one's family members as "mother",
"father", "brother", "sister", and so on was not a mere fiction. Quite apart from the
increased demands made upon the students' capacity for empathy, the language skills
required for these situations were at a much higher level. The following quote reflects
the experience of many:

Saturday, I don't know if I feel as if I've been here a long time
or hardly here at all. Such a bombardment of situations, impres-
sions and feelings and facts. In the past few days, only since Monday, I have been here! I have experienced some of the most intense
anxiety I have ever felt as well as excitement, frustration, enjoy-
ment, hunger bewilderment, ambivalence and strengths.

3) Ongoing Strain of Alienation

The demand to speak a language in which one has little facility creates a good deal of strain even in the classroom situation - and a wish to revert to a more comfortable situation in which words come naturally and with ease. Here are some examples:

> First Spanish lesson. This morning made me more anxious, feeling stupid, slow, than I have felt in ages. Do I have a barrier to language?

> The Spanish teacher has patience, friendliness, respect for us. ...at one point I felt like fleeing and having a good cry, but I stayed, so my better instincts prevailed and conquered. I desperately wanted D to write these things on the blackboard.

> Now I can relate to Puerto Ricans coming to New York and relating to fast-talking New Yorkers...

Another felt that:

> Being bombarded with a foreign language for eight hours in a classroom sitting and then in a social atmosphere at home can be very taxing. Concentration in depth is required at all times. There were times during the week when I wanted to sit quietly and converse leisurely with someone in English.

Even with increasing ability to understand, students felt the tension involved in learning a new language:

> I feel the day was worthwhile but there is a time limit on the amount of comprehending I can do. After a while the sounds become one big blur.

A student who knew some Spanish observed:

> I was overwhelmed by the Spanish. I couldn't believe how little I understood. I had thought that I knew some Spanish. I was angry, embarrassed, and lost all at once. Many people in Puerto Rico understand English, but they generally speak only Spanish.

> Things got worse. Acute frustration was added to my anger, embarrassment and confusion. I really wanted to understand and discuss various things.

With time the students began to recognize their conscious or unconscious feeling that English is "better" than Spanish:

> Also, on the radio today on the way to the beach, I heard Perry Como sing in Spanish. I suppose it's an instilled form of American chauvinism but it was strange to hear him sing in Spanish, as if English was somehow first.

Most often, the need to feel at ease speaking in one's native tongue was satisfied in student get-togethers. But on occasion a student might find that his competence in English could be used to help a Spanish-speaking family member. In the following example, that student not only had the satisfaction of being in the teaching/helping role which was part of her professional identity, but she also learned something about language:

> I helped M write her application for medical school (the essay in English). That took hours. I loved it. Being able to help someone else is important when you have been the one who always needed help. It also gave me an idea of the parts of the English language that are hard to learn (as a second language) and the necessary subtleties that are so difficult to express in a language not your own. For example M kept writing the word "must" when she meant "in order that", "it would be a good idea if", etc. As a result the essay had an authoritarian tone which is not her personality.

4) Trying Oneself Out

As linguistic skills were developed, however slowly, the need to try them out emerged. Naturally enough, this was often an attempt to marry the professional skills of a social worker with those of a speaker of Spanish. These attempts could be a chastening experience even in the later training cycles where far fewer demands were made upon the students as far as field work with clients was concerned. For example:

> After church we stop at the drug treatment center which is near the church. I had asked the mother if we could do this. Am surprised that she has remembered. Also realizing I am putting her in an unfamiliar position - feel honored that she has brought me here. Embarrassing for me. Realize that my Spanish is not good enough to understand - will have to come back when it is better. Feel very silly. Make excuse (which is true) that I must attend classes - do not have time now to visit but will when I talk with the rest of the group.

5) Understanding of Linguistic Variation

The Spanish the students learned in class at the Learning Center from their Puerto Rican or other Hispanic teachers was the standard language as it is spoken in Puerto Rico - a dialectal form derived from the language spoken in southern Spain. By and large, this was also the language spoken by the professionals whose lectures at Catholic University the students attended, and by the agency personnel and social service executives and planners whom they met.

In the lower social level families and neighborhood in which the students were placed, yet different dialectal variations were spoken (including local variations such as the speech of Playa de Ponce). In many ways, this lower-class Spanish might be compared to "black" English - the dialectal variation of the English language developed by southern blacks and now often encountered by social workers in New York City.

The students were obviously so busy just trying to learn any Spanish at all that they could not be sensitized much to such variation. However, they did develop some awareness of speech differences. From the reports of at least some students, it would appear that they gained first-hand experience of socio-linguistics. They knew "good" English from "bad". But they did not know "good" Spanish from "bad". They only knew that they had to learn the kind of Spanish that would help them get along and across in their temporarily adopted culture. It may well be that this experience will help them to contribute in a meaningful way to the current disputes about language in the New York City school and social service systems - not only in the current efforts toward bilingualism, but also, more generally, in a more tolerant attitude toward linguistic variation.

Footnotes:

1. D. Tendler. <u>Social Service Needs in a Changing Community: A Study of the Use of Voluntary Social Agencies by Puerto Rican Clients.</u> Unpublished Doctoral dissertation. (New York: New York University, 1965).

2. C. Garcia. <u>Study of the Initial Involvement in the Social Services by the Puerto Rican Migrants in Philadelphia.</u> (Philadelphia: Vantage Press, 1971).

3. The course was taught by Ms. Leticia Romero, M.S.W., Puerto Rico School of Social Work; faculty member SEEK program in the City University of the City of New York.

4. This course was taught by Mr. J. Ruiz of the Hunter College Spanish Department.

CHAPTER 13

EXPERIENCES WITH SELECTED FAMILY BELIEFS, ATTITUDES AND BEHAVIORS

A. EDUCATION

Our students found that education was seen as a value and an end in itself. That is, it was desirable and important to have an education, and this seemed to be status giving in a variety of ways. "The parents who don't have much education send all of their children to school."

The father is 52 years. He was born in the town not far from Ponce. He only attended school for three years then left to work in farming. He has lived in Ponce for over 30 years. For 27 years he has worked for the same company. He operates a machine punch. Although he does not speak English, he knows a few words for objects and enjoys pointing them out. He speaks of his lack of schooling with a mixture of pride and wistfulness that I have seen in several other men of similar circumstances. I sense a feeling of pride in accomplishing so much (family, job, house, car, etc.) through his own efforts without the help of education. This in my opinion is something truly to be proud of. It shows a consistency and dedication to life and family over a long period of time. However, there is a wistfulness, I think, for two reasons: 1) he did not have the opportunity to achieve something that society today values very highly, education. He grew up in a time and place when this was not as true as it is today; 2) I think he also misses on a personal level the knowledge he would have gained in going to school.

D is studying English in school and her mother helps her with her English homework (I do too and she helps me with my Spanish).

When mothers were asked about their aspirations, they gave high priority to the education of their children. Some saw education expressly as the path to upward mobility.

J, 19, is a student at the Catholic University. He is studying business. He is friendly but a little reserved. I sometimes help him with his English lessons and during this time am able to talk about other topics too. He has a girl friend who is a student in the University of Puerto Rico campus here in Ponce. I can identify with J in many ways. He is the son of working class people who have made it a value that he to go college. He is going there in order to get a better job (white collar) than working in the streets climbing poles for the phone company.

In conversations, J has mentioned some political issues, especially the one of Puerto Rico's status. It seems as though he is beginning to think about these things. However, he was raised in this system and is on the threshold of making it in this one.

A number of young adult husbands and sons in the families with whom the students lived, were reported to be attending university courses at night. The content of the courses chosen was clearly vocationally oriented and related to the conscious use of education as a stepping stone to better employment. Most students described their families as upwardly mobile and "making it" or attempting to "make it" within the established economic system and to present themselves as relatively conservative on social and political issues.

MATERIAL POSSESSIONS AND OUTWARD APPEARANCE

Material possessions as status symbols were frequently mentioned. It was observed by both the students and visiting faculty that even among households in which the income was quite limited, there was often an expensive television and stereo record playing equipment. Installment buying seemed to be widespread.[2]

A number of the families lived in the relatively recently constructed lower middle-class housing development called urbanizaciones. This kind of move sometimes required that both husband and wife be employed.

The family has lived in an urbanizacione since last December. This urbanizacione is a large, new development of concrete homes. The home contains 6 rooms and 2 bathrooms, including a formal dining room. The home is quite nicely furnished and equipped, including a color television and exercise bike, electric coolers, etc. The family also has a car and both Mr. and Mrs. R drive.

The observed concern with the possession of material goods is at some variance with the sometimes described high value placed on things spiritual in Puerto Rico.[3] The emphasis on outward appearance included an emphasis on dress, neatness and cleanliness in public places for both men and women.[4]

One student reinforced the need for material possessions as being true not only for the people in urbanizaciones but for many others as well.

In the family I lived with there were two refrigerators (1 worked); three clocks (none worked) and three TV sets (1 worked), and a record player which did not work. What appeared to be important was not whether these worked, but that the family had them on display.

VISITING

Respect for parents and elders including members of the extended family was frequently noted. A major social activity and obligation was observed to be the visiting of kin, and being visited by relatives and friends.[5]

When the family visits relatives in the country, mother, father, oldest son, myself and sometimes oldest daughter go. The rest remain in Ponce. We visited the country often. The brother of the mother lives there with his family - his wife and at least ten kids, probably more. They live on the side of a hill which must be climbed in order to reach the tin roof house. The brother grows his own food and raises animals but not commercially.

At different times...hordes of people would come to the house when we would eat lechon asado, arroz con habichuelas, etc. We drank pitorro. The men would go together and sing their decimas; the women would look on or help in the kitchen. Any topic was picked for the decima.

FAMILY SEX ROLES

The respective roles of men and women in the family are important elements in Puerto Rican life, and were observed by our students. "A good wife takes care of her husband, children and house." And, "a good wife is a good mother, loves her children, respects her husband." Greater freedom in social and sexual life was clearly permitted and expected in men.[6] There exists a very strong sense of responsibility for children by their fathers, whether this father is in the household or outside of the household. Children born in or out of wedlock are valued and fathers who live elsewhere because of separation or divorce are still expected to support and be in contact with their children and were described as doing so. The role of the man as the provider who takes responsibility for his children was frequently remarked. "A man takes care of his family." A good husband supports his wife and children, teaches them discipline and respect.[7]

The outward appearance of happiness as the desired public facade was reported.

> ...there is a big value of being or appearing happy here. For example, the Latinos at the Learning Center telling me how happy my landlady is, etc. Many of the people I've met in Ponce look less, much less, than happy. If in fact this is the case, it must be very difficult for the people. They would think there is something wrong with them if they're not happy. The culture wouldn't allow them to be in touch with or show their unhappiness - in the North American ways of showing it. Another case in point, was the party at Hogar Crea (therapeutic community) with the addicts. Everyone talking rapidly, smiling and laughing, singing. I'm not so sure that that type of activity indicates "happiness" at all. (It indicates expected behavior?)

The high value accorded peace and harmony in the household, or the facade of tranquility, came up a number of times and seemed to be related to the desirability of appearing to be "happy". It was mentioned as a goal of marriage to the students and supported by the findings of Tumin.[8] This value also appeared in the finding that family disagreements should be avoided.

NEORICANS (Puerto Ricans who live on the mainland.)

Neoricans were often viewed with distrust and distaste upon their return to Puerto Rico.

> The relatives of the family had spent time in Chicago; in fact, cousins of the kids in the family grew up in Chicago and were now living in Ponce. They knew Spanish adequately. The family always considered them Americans; they were into drugs and minor robberies. They were too scared to get really involved because they felt everyone knew exactly what they were doing (and they were right). My family never trusted them - locked all the doors in the house but accepted them because "they were family".

> Neoriquenos were considered the cause of the drug problem. They brought drugs back from the States. In fact, they seemed to be the brunt of all problems - they were the whipping boys. One could always spot a Neoriqueno - if he looked Rican and was wearing dungarees or "odd" clothing he was Neoriqueno.

For the young Neoriqueno returning, often with little knowledge of Spanish, it was not easy.

Decided to visit B and her family. C ("brother") who often takes
a walk at night offers to walk me. I invite him to come visit
the family with me. A lot of people are visiting when we arrive.
C mentions that he is taking a Spanish course. The room becomes
silent. "Why take a course in Spanish if you are a Puerto Rican?"
C - "I lived in New York for 18 years." He becomes increasingly
uncomfortable. It is obvious at the end of this small talk that C
does not know much Spanish and is unclear about his cultural identity -
he is neither a New Yorker nor a Puerto Rican Islander.

C later explains that the people with whom we visited initially
thought that I was the Puerto Rican and he the North American because I talked in Spanish more than he.

Some Neoricans identified themselves as essentially North Americans and with all
things North American. As a guest at a wedding, a student reported:

After a while, a young man came over to me and said, "What is a
New Yorker doing in a place like Ponce?" (in English). He is a
Neorican, 23 years old who grew up in New York and Philadelphia.
He came back for a few months to see his family, but had a plane
ticket to San Francisco. He really put down Puerto Rico and Puerto
Ricans. Never dates Puerto Rican girls, etc. I found myself de-
fending Puerto Rico. I felt he was being too harsh. He was very
much into making money and having "the good life". I also sensed
a lot of ambivalence and, yes, anger.

FEMININE BEAUTY

In Puerto Rico as in some other areas of the world, the model of female pul-
chritude is not the tall, slender form, and this surprised the female North American
students. While a degree of plumpness by North American standards was what the students found to be the locally desirable womanly appearance, it must be noted that
the starchy diet of Puerto Rico makes this something which can be readily achieved
if one has enough food. Thus, it also becomes an indication of affluence and being
"cared for".

M and her husband (the rich relatives) are fat. She made no bones
about her weight and told me she weighed 170 lbs. But she sat down
and ate rice and beans, potatoes, bread, boiled bananas, and some
fried pork. Her husband did the same. There is such a value in my
own social strata and culture on being thin!

UPWARD MOBILITY STRIVING

Not all values with which families were identified were free of conflict.

This family seems to me to be a mobility, status-conscious one.
They are concerned with material acquisitions and in some ways
seem stereotypically middle-class Americans. Perhaps there are
some value conflicts between traditional Puerto Rican values and
those of the aspiring middle class. As an example of this, P told
me that while he goes to school four nights a week (a sign of
mobility consciousness), he saves Friday night for being out for
beer and the boys (a traditional Puerto Rican custom).

Here the student has described the pull between a traditional social custom and the individual's mobility strivings.

> The mother proudly announced to me that English was always her favorite subject and that she wants her daughter to do well in it.

In this instance, the mother has really committed herself to the use of English, frequently seen as a step in upward mobility, since a knowledge of English, may result in employment in the local office of a North American corporation. Aside from this pragmatic issue, there are conflicting pulls between the local customs and traditions. The use of the Spanish language and the notion of independence of North American influence is at one extreme, and the study of English, employment with North American or multi-national corporations as the route to upward mobility, and political incorporation as a State with the United States, is at the other extreme. Opposing political views are openly discussed and taken very seriously in Puerto Rico.

OTHER VALUE CONFLICTS

Another kind of conflict as experienced by one student in the household in which he lived was described:

> There was a "generation conflict" in Ponce. The parents moved from the country village, to the city, Ponce. Though a lot of the kids spent time in the village, they really considered Ponce their home. The parents considered the village their home. (Puerto Rico is pueblo centered - one of the problems in defining island policy is this rivalry between pueblos.) This divides parents and children. The parents adapted to city life; the children basically knew nothing else and hated the country; the parents longed to return to the country. Another divising factor or symptom of the division was the music - the young crowd had the salva; the old crowd had the traditional libaro music of the country - and no dancing. Because that was wrong, in this family.

B. **FAMILY ROLES**

In "An Essay in the Definition of National Culture"[9] Mintz reported on a number of studies describing the child-rearing patterns in Puerto Rico. There seems to be general acceptance that despite variations from class to class and possibly even region to region, in all classes, obedience and respeto are the most universal expected qualities of children.

The expectations for boys and girls respectively, however, are quite different. Girls are expected to be submissive, boys are encouraged to be independent and aggressive. Children are invariably found to be closer to their mothers than to their fathers.

However, as with all generalizations, there are exceptions:

> Tonite as we were eating E, age 8, wanted to go out but she was told she couldn't by both her mother and father. She stormed out, went to her room and slammed the door. Her father scolded her and said he would tie her in her room if she tried to go out but he said it half-heartedly. As he left the room, Doña J came over to me and whispered conspiratorially that her husband spoils E because she is the only girl. She claims she takes care of all the physical discip-

lining of all her children. Her husband never hits any of them.

The student did, however, observe the differential status of the oldest son, who played a particular kind of role with certain responsibilities and perogatives.

> Children were very accommodating. Eldest son did the cooking since mother is sick. I washed the dishes.

The special status and roles in a variety of areas quickly emerged.

> The eldest son although only 18 has assumed the role of protector and family guardian. It doesn't seem to cause him any undue emotional strain and he plays his role with confidence and ease. Evidently his sleeping in the same room as his mother is another way of demonstrating his position as head of the household. Despite his position with his siblings, he shows great respect for his mother and defers to her decision if need be.

> She (mother) will share a room with P, her 24 year old son (the largest room). Her husband has a room, A another, then me. In the old house there were only 3 rooms and everything seemed fine - I'm not sure why four created so many problems. Also, it is not uncommon here I understand for the responsible son of the family to share a room with the mother. Not an indication of some underlying neurosis.

There is an expectation that the sons assume responsibility for the girls in the family, primarily for their safety and "chastity". One student who was dating a Puerto Rican girl learned that frequently a brother served as chaperone. This responsibility was often extended, as least in part, to the students who lived in the home.

> Eldest son very protective of me, will not leave home if I'm to be alone.

Unmarried children are expected to live in their parents' household until they are married.

> M who is 22, and J, her older brother who is 23, both live at home. It's my understanding that this is still generally the way it goes in Puerto Rico.

However, the married children still maintain a close relationship with the family and maintain very frequent contact.

> All of their children are married and live outside the home. However, their oldest son, R, visits the home daily. But C takes care of mostly all the household problems.

> Today we moved to an <u>urbanizacione</u>. We started at about 8 A.M. Neighbors, cousins and kids from the neighborhood came to help. C, the oldest son who lives with his wife and children, arrived in white tennis shorts but, in what I figure is his regular fashion, he did no work. He did carry some of us over to the new house in his car, then sped off with his neat cool self intact. No one seemed to resent this.

98

Family responsibilities were observed to be consistently allocated, although not always as overtly as expected.

When we first got to the house, it appeared as though this family was not very typical of the Latin family stereotype. M did not seem very forceful and there wasn't an apparent order to the way things were done.

However, after a month and more, I am able to see more clearly how the family functions.

M really is the head of the household. He is the wage earner and provider. He and society have delegated to B (mother) the job of running the house and raising the children. This is why she is the one who seems to be making decisions.

One time B told us that they had moved to their present house because of the large garden which she liked. However, a few years ago the government began planning to knock down all the houses in the area for a project. After hearing of this M has not done any further work on the house. The yard is overgrown and the house is in a poor state of repair. B is angry about this but she has not said anything to M about it because he is the boss. This has to be seen within the context of the Latin family.

C.   SEX ROLES

North American sex role definitions are in a process of changes which seem to vary substantially with race, ethnicity and social class. Among graduate students as a group, the civil rights movement, the women's movement and changing social events have found a ready response and produced considerable militancy for equality of opportunity and status for both sexes.

The graduate students who went to Puerto Rico varied in attitudes on sex discrimination from relative acceptance of conventional definitions to strongly racial feminist. Some were merely the products of accultruation in New York and had consciously strong views on sex role differentiation. In preparation for the Puerto Rico venture, there was considerable discussion in general, descriptive and anecdotal terms of what constituted the conduct standards of ladylike and gentlemanly behavior in this more formal society. Relevant readings were also assigned.

On arrival in Puerto Rico, lack of clarity about specifically appropriate, expected and accepted behaviors was a major cause of discomfort. Nowhere was this more apparent than in relation to sex roles.

Sex Role Induction of Female Students

The female students, as North American women, experienced the greater discomfort. In both verbal and written reports women students expressed their distress at the behavior of men toward them in public places, that is while out walking on the street, visiting a public beach and the like. They were uncomfortable about how men looked at them, and about the sounds and cat-calls made in their direction which they did not perceive as acceptable and appropriate behavior. They made frequent reference to being talked to and looked at - up and down - by the men they passed on public thoroughfares or who drove by in their cars. While they frequently did not understand the exact wording of the remarks in their direction, the manner, tone and gesture with which they were delivered were unmistakable. They were aware

99

very quickly that they were not being singled out for this treatment, but that this was a male response to women from adolescense to middle age.

> I have been walking to and from the Center, at least one way per day, if not both ways. It helps me to get to know the streets better because there is literally no other opportunity to do so, especially after dark. I still have a bit of trepidation about walking through or near the groups of young men and boys that congregate on the corners and the corner bars...there is the direct stare of the men that is sometimes uncomfortable. I still feel "how dare they!"

One of the sounds the women students found annoying came from local male puckered lips, like a series of kisses. The remarks coming from individuals and groups of men varied widely from mild equivalence of "hello beautiful" to especially sexually colored statements:

> ...asked if it was alright for me to go bowling with L (child), H said yes but she didn't want to go because the men said things to her about how sexy and big her behind is.

Also somewhat unnerving were the cars driven by males which slowed down, sometimes to the pace of the student's walk, and continued along the curb with the men making a variety of remarks and offering a variety of propositions and invitations. While this sometimes slowed traffic on busy streets, the other drivers of vehicles, mostly men, seemed quite tolerant of this and there was no unusual honking of horns.

Both observation and discussion with female Puerto Rican exchange students made it clear that this manner of looking at women and making comments to them was acceptable behavior among Puerto Ricans rather than unusual behavior and that women who grew up in this culture did not necessarily define it as provocative or undesirable. The reaction of a number of Puerto Rican young women who were graduate students in New York to this discussion was: "We like it", and that they would be disappointed if some remarks were not made in their direction by men on the street in their accustomed surroundings in Puerto Rico.

Both the acute personal discomfort, and the observations of the acceptability of the sex role behaviors quickly disabused even the more radical feminists among the students of any ideas of initiating change among the women of Puerto Rico during their three month stay in Ponce.

Sex Role Differentiation

Sex role differentiation was observed to start early in Puerto Rico:

> I observed in my community that boys of all ages are given unlimited freedom to come and go and visit. For girls it is quite different. Even the little girls are restricted to the front of their homes within mother's vision. Being out alone and after 7 P.M. is frowned upon for grown women.

> ...visited the local swimming pool. There don't seem to be many female visitors. Evidently girls are not allowed at the pool except accompanied by older siblings or relatives.

Another student, remarking about the family with whom he lived, noted:

100

The daughters are not allowed to go out unescorted; usually two go together. If M and P (father and mother) go out, they like us (student and wife) to stay home with the girls.

Personal freedom for boys and restriction for girls in Puerto Rican child rearing is reported in various publications.[10]

The women students began to learn quickly that women are not supposed to be on the streets during the evening.

I had to go get cigarettes and I asked if that was okay - I'm not sure if A accompanied me for company or because women are supposed to have someone with them after dark.

It became very clear that being on the streets alone at night was an invitation to be called "puta" or whore, and to be openly accosted. It also became clear that in public places women were expected to be accompanied either by other women or by their children (e.g., married women) or by men. A number of students reported having been called "gringa y puta", North American whore, while walking on the streets during the day alone.

The student living with one family reported:

Outside the church, the oldest and youngest girls had no activities - except their household chores. The oldest was a slave; she cooked, ironed, cleaned, entertained. She was the second mother in the house, 30 years old and single. The youngest worked in a beauty parlor that she owned and spent her nights at church activities.

Both our students living with families in barrios and Puerto Rican young women who were their "sisters" in the families with whom some lived sought ways to avoid the restrictions to get out of the house at night.

Visit another student at her home. Meet her family. Her "sister" offers to make me a second "sister" - implies that it is only by having these "American sisters" that she can get out as frequently as she does. Very different from my own life in New York!

Later...find two project students and the "sister" of one sitting on the wall with the abuela and C. All amiable chatting. I am delighted. Very much want my "family" to know the group. Will also make it easier for me to get out at night.

The mother in one barrio household summarized the life of a married woman in Puerto Rico with the statement "with marriage a woman loses many of her rights; she must stay at home and take care of her husband and children and should never talk to other men.[11] Another phrased it: "A woman has many responsibilities: she has to worry about food, money, children and make her husband happy."

The women students were startled by the overt attention paid them by male relatives and friends of the families with whom they lived as they struggled with defining appropriate sex roles for themselves. They expected these male relatives and friends to assist them with understanding the appropriate behavior and to help them be inducted to the proper role, rather than to relate to them as women who are potential conquests.

The "brother" of the student I visited drives H and me home. His baby and H sit in the back. As he leaves me at the door - flirtatiously (I think) says to tell other student when I will next be there. Will be there too. I am startled he is married. Has a child. <u>Machismo</u> at work?

The young men were very attentive to M and me and usually behaved respectfully. I think because of my "brothers". My handsome neighbor S came onto me but soon realized sweet phrases were not getting him anywhere, and switched to being agreeable without "the line". But some of the older men were more puzzling. My "father's" brother followed M and me to our table continuing to talk. He keeps calling his wife - the old lady. And later when I was scratching my mosquito bites asked me to scratch his back. I nearly started to - then stopped and said, no. He kept asking, why, and I couldn't think of the words in Spanish - all I could think of was I'm afraid and S was nearby so I talked to him. M had her own similar problems. We talked about it later and decided what was so troubling was that in such a family gathering we'd expect the older men to refrain from putting us in a bad position - in fact to guide us in proper etiquette. Instead it was often impossible to know what was innocent and what was not.

What I think though is in the future we should stay more with wives and try to find out what's proper from them. The obstacle to this is that the wives seem to be less inclined to deal with our Spanish. Anyway we'll have to take the chance of offending the men (when the situation is not clear). The best option here seems to be the most conservative one.

The deference to men in the household was frequently noticed.

When K (father), C (eldest son) or M (son) want anything, they just ask for it. Sometimes this takes on a very harsh aspect such as when C sits at the table and yells to his mother to serve him his food and stop talking to someone. Most of the time there is not much conflict. The women seem to accept this at least on the surface.

Sometimes T goes to a nearby bar to play billiards and doesn't return till well after dinner. He immediately demands his dinner and gets it. Even though M complains about his staying out to us or other family members, nothing is said to T when he returns.

A male student observed:

There was a great deal of resentment against <u>machismo</u> among the girls of this family. They were tired of the men getting all the goodies - as they saw it - and the women getting all the work. This caused a great deal of anger in them which somehow could not be vented because they knew of no alternatives. The result was pervasive depression among the women in this family. Ironically, the boys in the family were angry because they felt that the women were controlling their lives, in religion, dating. Yet they could not - except in minor ways - really change this. The result was a greater attempt to act machismo - a false resolution. Yet none of the boys in the family would claim to be macho since it would arouse the anger of the girls in the family.

102

It is not suggested that all women are conflicted about their subservient role to male authority. When asked directly what they would change about their husbands if they could make changes, the most frequent reply was "nothing". This kind of reply may reflect the prescription that it is not proper to complain about one's husband, and that, indeed, such complaints may reflect on the wife, too. It has been suggested that sometimes a woman, "...may even tend to exaggerate his dictatorial masculinity and portray herself as a masochistic victim in the hands of a strong, virile tyrant,[12] rather than admit that her man is not macho. Thus women support aggressive masculinity amidst lamentation, since it validates their saintly status.

Sex Role Induction of Male Students

Newly arrived male students in some instances began their induction into the locally expected male behavior by being instructed by their barrio household mothers to go to the corner bar to drink and to talk with the neighborhood men who congregate at the bar, the usual male hang-out. This was expected male behavior. The deference shown males in each household, has already been described.

Observation and discussion with the male visiting students suggested that they were not all comfortable with the more sexually male role than the one into which they had been socialized in their own life experience up to this point. To the best of our knowledge none of the male students engaged in the verbal and non-verbal, more aggressive male sexual manifestations discussed earlier. The male students were fewer in number and some seemed to take some pleasure from the local culture of male superiority, despite their individual discomfort at times with this role cast. They tended to "play-along" with the cues from their "family" in a modest fashion, to retreat to the background and to be less engaged with some aspects of family life.

Social Behavior: Male/Female

Some of the men students tried dating local girls and experienced the chaperone system with curiosity and discomfort. One student's comment:

My "family" discussed dating in Ponce, and there are still many instances where couples have to have a chaperone (Wow! What price virginity, machismo, etc.) M brought up an interesting point saying that when her younger brother (18) started dating a girl, she (M) couldn't be the chaperone because she was too young and not known by the family. However, had she been known by the family she would not be considered too young and could have chaperoned the couple. But older people can always be chaperones whether or not they are known by the family.

Hill's study of courtship patterns in Puerto Rico suggested that the chaperone system led to early marriages and served as a control and protection of girls from promiscuity and slander.

One of the male students dated a local girl and reported the sequence of relatives from parents to siblings who joined the party as chaperone on dates.

A quite different form of highly structured male/female conduct free from family supervision and control in a public night club was remarked upon by several who participated. The contrast with more accustomed street behavior is so very apparent.

Tonite was interesting, (two other students) and I were planning to go to the Club (this time for dancing) so when I told M she

103

made up my face with her make-up and I didn't have the heart to wash my face. I had orange eyeshadow over my eyes, red on my cheeks in great big circles and red on my lips. Then, I figured it would be dark in the club...

I went to the Club and danced with what seemed to be thirty different men. First they came to your table where you are seated with your girl friends (there were six of us, 3 Puertoricans) and if you refuse, I was told, you can't dance with anyone else for that dance or there may be a fight between the two men. Then they escort you to the dance floor to only Latin music and dances and then you're escorted back to your chair til the next dance. There were two men from Spain there who didn't go through those routines. Many of the men were married. It was my first real look at the macho phenomenon. None of the women leave with any of the men. If the man is interested they both say when they will be at the Club again and agree to see each other then. The women we were with seemed primarily concerned with how good-looking the men were. "Muy guapo" was the line we heard over and over again.

After shopping, my "sister" and I got ready to go out. We picked up several of her girl friends and went to the Club. I definitely felt the culture shock because it was, for me, such a different scene than I'm used to. Even my clothes were pale and "straight" in comparison. The women wore quite a lot of make-up and wore pantsuits, dressy ones, and hairpieces, and much jewelry. The women are known at this Club, and the flow of people around us was nice. The men are, in a way much more formal than what I'm used to but definitely friendly. They were all interested in dancing and I even succeeded in learning the meranque. After a dance, my partner would escort me back to my table and pull out my chair! No one drank very much, some not at all, and I was amazed we could sit and talk without being hassled to buy drinks. I was a bit nervous - here I am - I don't know anything about Latin music (and it was all Latin music) nor the dances nor much Spanish after only a couple of days. Besides, the group spoke muy rapido and in many idioms, but after a while I just relaxed and had a hell of a good time. I even had a date with a student from the Catholic University on Wednesday.

And the contrast with student social experience in New York:

Here I am dancing Latin dances with Puerto Rican men who are so far removed from the men I date in New York. I could see the man I left in New York with his shoulder-length hair, long mustache, Marine Corps tatoo, patched jeans, and t-shirt, also on this same Friday night, dancing to American rock music and acting in his totally New Yorkese way with the women he is meeting. And a few weeks ago, that was my lifestyle too - the style of Woodstock and a pushing of the limits of freedom we have. And now, I'm wearing make-up, nail polish, acting a bit demure. It's all me, but it's mind-boggling to me right now. The dancing is senuous, but here again, it's another ambivalent message. Without being facetious do people here have sex? The men and women came to this Club separately, met, sat together, danced together, held hands, etc., but left separately. How different from my circle of friends in New York! As I see it now, this way is easier because the rules are fairly definite although not uncomfortably rigid. In New York, it seems we are making frameworks only to break them down.

104

Social Dress and Appearance

The New York visitors noted that the women dressing for social occasions prepared themselves in a style to which the New Yorkers were not accustomed. The clothing was described as more "flashy" and the wearing of heavy make-up, nail polish, and hair pieces was remarked upon.

"The clothes she likes are the 'sexy' clothes."

Everyone here (young women) dresses-up, wears make-up and seems so colorful that by comparison I look washed-out and pale in total appearance.

A physical closeness among women to which they were not accustomed was also noticed and noted by some of the New York students.

Women here touch more and fuss over each other.

The male manner of dress was observed to be more conservative and formal for all occasions. White or pastel colored shirts, dark trousers and dark shoes was the usual attire, with the higher status persons wearing ties and jackets in addition as status symbols in their work establishments. Hairstyles were relatively short and always neatly combed. Slovenly dress, wearing patched clothing (e.g., the patches on bluejeans which are commonly worn), unkept hair or a scraggily beard are viewed as inappropriate. As one student summarized it:

Puerto Ricans dress consciously, they are neat and generally overdressed for the weather. Even the poorest dress cleanly and with self-respect.

A disheveled appearance is sometimes related to a disturbed state of mind by some Puerto Ricans. One male student who wore his hair at shoulder length, although it was generally tied back, was eventually asked to leave his housing in a public project by the "mother" who complained that his appearance was causing too much talk.

Another visiting male student who trimmed his hair and beard was then classified by the Puerto Rican group with whom he worked as "the saint" which placed him outside of usual conventions and which made it alright for him to have a beard. The rule of thumb became that persons who made a neat appearance even if they sported long hair or beards were generally acceptable while those who did not were more apt to get flak on the streets.

Difference Between Male and Female Student Experience

The general code of conduct expected of women and men has been loosely outlined as it was experienced by the visiting students who were being inducted into the roles of male and female young adults in this culture. Violations of the norms clearly held more danger for women than for men. Unaccompanied women tended to be defined as women inviting male attention and exploitation and therefore, fair game for anything. This was particularly true on the public beaches during the day and on the streets at night. Thus, non-conforming men might be the objects of ridicule and verbal hostility, but North American women, who were by appearance and dress usually identifiable, were classified as loose foreign women to begin with, and even small violations of the local dress codes or time codes (permissible hours on the street) might be viewed as invitation or provocation and produce responses which might vary from verbal abuse to sexual assault.

105

D. WORK ROLES

In their perception of the work roles performed by Puerto Ricans in New York, our students initially were probably not very different from the average New Yorker as described earlier. Most of the Puerto Ricans they ever knew were ghetto inhabitants holding blue collar or service jobs in downtown factories, in restaurants, apartment or office buildings and stores. Since all students also had some experience in the welfare and social service fields, they also knew many Puerto Ricans as clients of social agencies.

The orientation sessions offered before they left for Ponce were intended to broaden this perspective as much as possible within the limitations of time and the multiple orientation needs of the program. They learned to deal with Puerto Ricans who were vendors at the marketa, shopkeepers in bodegas and botánicas, or even espiritistas performing work roles as healers and advisors.

The orientation sessions quite naturally exposed them to a sizable number of people of the professional class, primarily social workers, mental health professionals and social scientists. For many students, this was the very first time that they had the experience of Puerto Ricans performing such roles, and the very first time that they were interacting with Puerto Ricans who were their teachers and supervisors rather than their waiters, servants or clients. Some students were well aware of the novelty of the situation, and even expressed their surprise to some of the Anglo members of the project staff. Perhaps this emerging awareness of their own stereotyping was the true beginning of their cross-cultural learning.

Of course the orientation process also served to confirm some prior perceptions, simply because they had a reality basis. The Puerto Rican professional class in New York consists of a relatively small number of men and women. Many of them are articulate spokesmen for the betterment of the status of Puerto Ricans in New York. But this highlights the fact that the Puerto Ricans, as a group, are still "outs" fighting to get "in". Their participation in actually governing the city and making the rules and decisions which affect the day-to-day life and the future of Puerto Ricans is still very limited. With some oversimplification, one can say that New York Puerto Ricans are governed, and are not governing much of anything except perhaps their own ghetto communities in very localized and circumscribed situations.

Observation of Work Roles in Ponce

The students' living with a Puerto Rican family gave them an opportunity to observe their "parents" and "siblings" in their day-to-day performance of a variety of work roles. In addition, they were involved to some degree in the life of the barrio and the larger urban community as a whole.

By and large, the students were placed in lower class to lower-middle-class families, so that their most intimate observations were of the work roles of this group.

Women's Work

Nearly all the "mothers" were amas de casa (housewives). For a fairly large minority, this was their exclusive occupation. At the risk of sounding trite, let us spell out what that involved. By and large, they fitted into a pattern familiar to North Americans: the husband went to work and was the breadwinner, and the wife stayed at home. A fairly typical routine would be for her to prepare breakfast for her husband and the student boarder before they went to work. Then the children were fed and sent to school. Pre-school infants, pets and sometimes chickens would then be tended. After that, the house was cleaned - a major task in Puerto Rico where cleanliness and tidiness is highly valued. Shopping for and preparing the evening meal would take up that part of the day which was not devoted to a multiplicity of other chores including the washing, mending or sewing of clothes, and so on. For example:

A is always doing something: cooking, washing dishes, doing Mac-rame, etc. She is up doing something from 6 A.M. until about 10 P.M. Monday through Friday. On Saturdays she likes to sleep late.

Quite a few women added to their workload in ways which would not take them away from home. Taking in student boarders was, naturally, the example observed most often in our program. Some women had been doing this for years, often taking more than one boarder. Except for the fact that the boarders were Anglos, this seemed to be a pattern fairly close to the Puerto Rican extended family system, where caring for children and adults related by blood, friendship or compadrazgo is common enough. For example:

A man entered the house, sat at the table and also ate. He, I learned, is a boarder living in an extension of the home with his disturbed brother. M has had several Peace Corps volunteers stay with her in the past.

Other women might operate a small store (tiendita) in or near the house. For example:

P runs a small shop in a kind of small shed behind the house. She sells sandwiches, cold drinks, ices, etc., mostly to young fellows who take vocational courses behind the house.

The majority of women, however, were holding part-time or full-time jobs. The jobs encountered most frequently were: factory worker, clerical worker and nursing. For the most part these jobs did not relieve the women from the task of running the house and tending to the children, although there sometimes was a live-in relative or neighbor to help out with these tasks.

Occasionally one of our women students might be asked to pitch in - a request which was met, as a rule, more or less gracefully. For example:

(the mother) came in at 7 P.M. and started to wash the floors. I offered to help so I cleaned the dining room floor while (mother) fixed my dinner of rice and beans and meat and salad and Coca Cola... (The son) was out delivering papers but his meal was waiting for him.

We noted that in our whole sample of "mothers", there was only one who was living on welfare. She was a single parent with five children.

Men's Work

The men's work roles were observed less closely than the women's for the reason that the men's jobs took most of them outside of the home.

The majority of men were blue-collar workers holding a variety of jobs in local factories and construction firms. Quite a few of them used their skills -

especially carpentry, plastering and painting - to take additional work for pay or to improve their own homes. For example:

> G (father, about 50 years old) is a carpenter. He has a job at
> a factory and earns $100 gross per week. He works Monday through
> Friday until about 4:30 P.M. But he works at least 4-5 additional
> hours each evening. He has his own shop and has made a lot of fur-
> niture in his home. At this time, the house is undergoing expansion;
> G and some of his friends are doing a lot of the work.

This pattern of self-help and neighborhood sharing of skills and tasks was obser-ved quite often not only in the families with whom our students lived, but in all the barrios. Helping relatives or neighbors with projects that they could not do all by themselves seemed to be a natural thing to do; something that was expected of one, and something that one had a right to expect of others.

We might note that construction and maintenance skills have been one of Puerto Rico's "exports" to New York City where Puerto Rican neighborhoods abound in carpentry and repair shops which in turn cater to their fellow Hispanics engag-ed in building maintenance. And while a current TV comedy series may get a few chuckles out of viewers who hear a Hispanic superintendent protest that something or other "eez not mai chob", chances are that helpfulness and cooperation are found far more often - especially, of course, if the person requesting help is him-self Hispanic and therefore has a kind of claim within the prevailing cultural pattern.

A number of the men in our students' "families" were white collar workers: store clerks, bookkeepers and so on. Only a very few were in the professions, but this was in part a consequence of our criteria in selecting the families from the lower and lower-middle class levels.

E.   RELIGION

Puerto Rico is a Catholic country. The Puerto Rican form of Catholicism has been described as "womb to tomb" religion, with the Church involved in baptism, confirmation, weddings and last rites. However, one does feel the religiosity of the people even outside the Church.

Most of the students, in describing the homes in which they lived, referred to the frequent presence of religious pictures of Christ and of Mary, of crucifixes and of figurines of saints.

Religious holidays and festivals are important to the Puerto Rican family.

Several of the students, in describing their families, referred to the fact that though the family was ostensibly "Catholic", some members of the family be-long to other groups, e.g., Pentecostal, or were non-practicing.

As an example of a family where the religion was important, but with accept-ance for those for whom it was not, the following example is offered:

> One of the first things which pops into my mind and impressed me a
> great deal was the totally dominating role which the Catholic Church
> played with this family. The carriers of the religion in the family
> were the women, with the mother as its chief lobbyist. Though the
> father was very devout, he could accept the dissentation by some
> family members around the existence of God.

All of the girls in the family had a strong faith in God and attended Church willingly. In fact, the 2nd oldest girl in the family was at this time a Nun in the States - midwest. Her existence, however was not mentioned to me until 6-7 weeks after I arrived. The girls talked about her with a lot of pride; the boys had a trace of disdain in their voices when speaking of her vocational choice. Two of the girls were deeply involved with the Church, e.g., Church activities, Sunday School. One was so involved and so wrapped up with the Church that she was mockingly called the Prophet of the family. Even the mother made fun of her. However, the mother went to Church every morning, waking at 5 A.M. to do so.

One of the boys, the University attender, questioned this belief in God and would discuss cautiously with the family. The girls in the family could not understand his behavior. They felt that he should just stop questioning and accept the fact that God exists. The mother was totally distraught, at her wit's end because she did not know what to do with her child. The father took a more benign attitude saying that he had shown his son the "way" and now it was up to him to accept it or not. He recognized that people who did not believe in God could still be "good". The boys in the family silently supported their brother since they were annoyed at having to attend church but would never renounce their faith in God.

The parish priest was a regular visitor to the house. He was young (39) and from Spain - a very opinionated, strong man with an uncanny insensitivity to the needs of his parishoners. The girls generally liked him though one did not. The boys hated him. He was a forceful, unbending, quite entertaining; a flirtatious young priest. He was both charming and insulting. He spent Christmas and New Year's Day with the family.

One might well wonder whether the weak hold of the Catholic Church on many Puerto Ricans might not be related to the fact that members of the clergy in Puerto Rico are frequently from North America or from Spain.

...(first Sunday) after breakfast, a shower, P suddenly appears in my room. "We are going to church now" - very surprised, I redress - into a shirt. No notice beforehand. I am very struck by how a lot is said or maybe not said in this house. The silence of this house. Especially at meals. Maybe because I am new.

Church - a surprise. Women in pants (C, who is not with us because he is working in the store for 1/2 day) explains that this is to protect them from the sun - he sounds sure but I am not. A priest who looks like an American, looks sweaty and bored. There is something pathetic about this congregation.

Moynihan and Glazer in describing the strength of the Pentecostal Church as compared to the Catholic Church in New York and Puerto Rican community note that the preachers and ministers of the Pentecostal Church are almost all Puerto Rican. They quote a member as saying:

In the Catholic Church no one knew me. Here if a stranger comes in, he is warmly greeted.[13]

This sentiment is described by one of the students in talking to a young boy in the family with which she was living.

P was describing to me how when he was about ten years old he began going to a Pentecostal Church. He liked the music and camaraderie there "in the Catholic Church no one knows you - you are a stranger - but in the Pentecostal Church everyone greets you. When you are sick they all come to the hospital to see you." He said he felt a coolness around his heart at some of the meetings and was told that he jumped about moved by the spirit. His mother accompanied him once and when she saw this she refused to let him go.

The house is a bustle of activity at 7:30 A.M. Church commences at 8:30 A.M. All members of the family are expected to attend. I accepted the invitation and attend services. Very interesting. The sermon was on the increase in crime - worldwide. The congregation as well as elders of the church seem to insist on lowered tranquil voices. I got the feeling of peace - at all costs. Somehow the congregation seemed almost without emotion - abnormal, I think. Or maybe in contrast to the loudness that is part of this way of life. They were quiet. I'm impressed with the number of youth. Religion is an integral part of this family. Respect for God, respect for parents.

The students who remained in Puerto Rico after December 15th, became involved in the excitement of the Christmas (Las Navidades) season, starting early in December and running through to January 6th, Three Kings Day.

Christmas is a time for visiting and eating and drinking.

Villancicos (carols) are sung, friends organize "parrandas", groups of roving merrymakers who go from house to house with asaltos (attacks or surprise visits) until all hours of the morning, waking their friends with boisterous singing and noisemaking.[14]

Together with the formal religion is the practice of Spiritualism which involves "the use of herbs and spiritist prayers, as well as professional or semi-professional practitioners who are consulted to cure illness, solve problems and cast spells.[15]

Certainly the many Botánicas in the area of the city inhabited by Puerto Ricans attest to the prevalence and strength of the belief.

If you ever talk to a Puerto Rican who says he doesn't believe in spirits, you know what that means, it means you haven't talked to him long enough.

This statement is attributed to a Puerto Rican in Dan Wakefield's Island in the City: A World of Spanish Harlem.

To quote a student who spent a great deal of time in a number of homes in Ponce:

I think it is important to emphasize how often formal religion and spiritualism are often intermixed, the continuing influence of the "pagan" on the Catholic household and how the twain do meet with little feeling of inconsistency on the part of the family. In one and the same house you can have the two existing together.

CONCLUSION

One of the most striking and frequent observations was the emphasis on education for the younger generation. This was true for the children; their school attendance and performance, and often their homework, were monitored quite closely by the parents. But it was also true for the young adults. Many of them attended extension or credit courses in areas which would help them get ahead in their field. A carpenter might take a course in draftsmanship and building construction, or a bookkeeper might be enrolled in an accounting degree program at the university.

At this level, the difference between the expectations for men and women was seen most clearly. A typical (and, to North Americans, familiar) example is the following:

> T (high school age son) stated during dinner that he expected to go
> to college and become a doctor, but that his sister would probably
> only get her B.S. and become a secretary since she would eventually
> marry. Neither T's sister nor his mother argued this point.

In many ways, then, our students were on fairly familiar territory when it came to work roles and expectations. The Puerto Rican families whose lives they shared were not all that different in this respect from mainland families of comparable socioeconomic level.

If the students had any lingering notions of Puerto Rico as a tropical paradise, they were quickly disabused of them when observing the strong commitment to an ethic of work, and the ambitions toward social mobility. We need hardly point out again how much this contrasts with so much of the welfare, mental health and social science literature discussed earlier, with its emphasis on marginality, social dysfunction and illness.

But there is an additional, perhaps critical, lesson our students learned. Through their studies at the Puerto Rico Learning Center and Catholic University, they became acquainted with a good many Puerto Ricans who were professors or who held executive positions in social work, government and industry. The contacts with members of the governmental structure often occurred in an atmosphere of formality which could be a bit intimidating to students accustomed to the more informal mainland manners.

The students thus had to unlearn their stereotype of Puerto Ricans as an underclass of immigrants governed by Anglos. The observation of work roles forced them as much as anything else to see Puerto Ricans in the social context of a self-governing community. They had to restructure their perceptions to fit a horizon of self-reliance, cultural and national pride. And this may well have been the most important cross-cultural experience with which the project began to acquaint them.

Footnotes:

1. Adler-Horton. et. al. A Study of Ten Puerto Rican Families. Unpublished Master's Project Report. (New York: Hunter College School of Social Work, 1974) p. 37-38.

2. This confirms Lewis' observations of the early 1960's. Ten years later every home has a TV, often a large color set. See Oscar Lewis, A Study of Slum Culture, op. cit., p. 105-106.

3. Lewis reported that clothing was a very important item in many households with the slum families he studies spending more on clothing than on all other items used, Ibid., p. 105.

4. Adler-Horton, et. al. op. cit., p. 26.

5. Ibid.

6. C. Senior. The Puerto Ricans: Strangers, then Neighbors. (Chicago: Quadrangle Books, 1965), p. 8-9.

7. Adler-Horton, et. al. op. cit., p. 28-29, 57.

8. Melvin Tumin and Arnold Feldman. Social Class and Social Change in Puerto Rico. (Princeton, N. J.: Princeton University Press, 1961), p. 250-56

9. Mintz. op. cit.

10. See discussion of child-rearing in: David Landy. Tropical Childhood. (Chapel Hill: University of North Carolina Press, 1959); S. W. Mintz. "Puerto Rico: An Essay in the Definition of Natural Culture." See: Child-rearing in: Status of Puerto Rico: Selected Background Studies for the U.S. - Puerto Rico Commission (Washington, D.C.: Government Printing Office, 1966), Mills, et.al. Puerto Rican Journey (New York: Harper, 1950); Elena Padilla. Up from Puerto Rico (New York: Columbia University Press, 1958) re: Child-rearing in New York Puerto Rican Community; J. M. Stycos. Family and Fertility in Puerto Rico (New York: Columbia University Press, 1955).

11. See descriptions of family life in: S. W. Mintz, "An Essay in the Definition of Natural Culture.", op. cit.; J. M. Stycos, op. cit., E. Padilla, op. cit.; Mills et. al., op. cit.; Glazer and Moynihan, Beyond the Melting Pot (Cambridge, Mass: M.I.T. Press, 1963), p. 88-90; M. Opler. Culture and Social Psychiatry (New York: Atherton, 1967), p. 381-82; E. Stevens, op. cit., p. 63.

12. Janet Adler-Horton, et. al. Ten Puerto Rican Families (New York: Hunter College School of Social Work, 1974), unpublished Master's thesis, p. 53; quoting Joseph Bram "The Lower Status Puerto Rican Family", (New York: Mobilization for Youth, March 1963), World of Education; School and Community Course. (Unpublished)

13. Moynihan and Glazer, op. cit., p.106

14. K. Wagenheim, op. cit., p. 222.

15. O. Lewis. A Study of Slum Culture. op. cit., p. 52.

16. D. Wakefield, Island in the City: A World of Spanish Harlem. (Boston: Houghton Mifflin, 1959).

SECTION III

THE OUTCOME OF THE PROJECT

INTRODUCTION

In evaluating the outcome of the project, the basic questions are:

    a) What have the students learned? and

    b) How have they been able to use their new knowledge in social work practice?

We tried to show above how Puerto Ricans are perceived by <u>Anglos</u> in a certain cognitive framework, and we suggested that this framework implies a negative attitude toward all or most things Puerto Rican. This ranges from the gross prejudice of our imaginary average New Yorker who dislikes or is afraid of <u>Spiks</u>, to the perception of economic disadvantage reflected in census data, to (very importantly for the social work professional) the subtle condescension expressed in so much of the social science literature.

We also indicated the problem of inadequate social work training in understanding the significance of cultural factors in dealing with a client group which comes from a different cultural background than that of the worker. We dealt with the special significance of communication and language in the inter-cultural approach.

We also tried to show through the students' own reports the learning process they had gone through in Puerto Rico.

We might, then, rephrase the initial questions as follows:

    a) How has their cognitive framework changed? and

    b) How has this change affected their social work practice?

These issues were explored by informal faculty-student discussions, feedback reports from the faculty field instructor, and a followup questionnaire in which the students were asked, among other things, to report critical incidents which seemed relevant to their Puerto Rican experience.

CHAPTER 14

SUMMARY

Following is a summary of our efforts, which seems to fall rather naturally into five groupings:

1. Culture shock of the barrio live-in experience.

2. Language skills.

3. Sex, family and work roles.

4. Problems of psychosocial diagnosis.

5. Respect for another people's culture.

Barrio Living and Culture Shock

The students' reports make it clear that the requirement of living with a
barrio family caused a sharp culture shock to most of them. Lack of familiarity with
customs and expectations and the lack of a language in which to even ask what was expected, hit some students very hard. Barrio living was strong medicine indeed. Whether it was also the best possible medicine is a question we cannot answer with assur-
ance without comparative studies and appropriate controls.

By and large, however, the students reported that the learning process had
had important results. They could now understand more readily some of the reactions
of Puerto Ricans immersed in New York City's Anglo culture; their disorientation, fear
and sometime hostility.

We also observed some examples of reverse culture shock. Some students,
upon their return, found it difficult to re-adapt to some of the demands and rules
of Anglo life in New York, especially as these were reflected in the regulation and
requirements of the School and the agencies in which they were placed, for the last
semester before graduation. We are not merely talking about a problem of discipline,
but about the project students' repeated efforts to convince faculty and fellow students that they had gone through some sort of arduous initiation. At times these
efforts were thinly disguised requests for special privileges, but most often they
seemed an attempt at getting across the idea that they had a story to tell - and an
important one not only to themselves but to the field of social work.

Understandably, a good part of the re-induction into the School's and the
agencies' business-as-usual procedures was resented by the students. This seems similar to the experience of many Peace Corps returnees. The rebelliousness of the group
was noted (with disapproval, needless to say) by quite a few faculty members. Feedback sessions with project faculty succeeded in composing some of the differences.

On the whole, our impression is that both the School and the agencies were
better off for having had to deal with some of this discontent.[1]

Language Skills

Over the three years of the project, we found it necessary to place increasing emphasis on the development of language skills. We realized during the first year

that even intensive spring-and-summer study could not prepare the student hitherto unacquainted with <u>el idioma</u> to do interviewing of individuals or groups in Spanish. As our group performed well above average on the Foreign Service Institute tests, we believe that this is a meaningful finding which should caution others engaging in similar projects against overly optimistic expectations.

However, our follow-up study showed that even a little Spanish can go a long way. To start with the most primitive level, that of professional self-interest, we found that a number of our project graduates were hired primarily because of their knowledge of Spanish. As for the more important level of client interest, we found that even poor language skills helped to establish rapport with clients and Spanish-speaking staff members. Says one student:

> I have excellent rapport with several Puerto Rican women, who have only marginal contact with our program, because I chat with them in limited Spanish.

We noted above the problem of access to agencies experienced by Puerto Ricans, and the problems of outreach experienced by agencies. Obviously language skills help in these situations. An example of work with an individual:

> In the hospital, in the methadone treatment program, I was able to contact a man's sister when he needed nursing home placement and she came in to see me because I spoke Spanish and wrote her a note in her language.

Another illustration in the community outreach area:

> While at the hospital, I was approached by a woman involved with a housing project in the catchment area. She and her group would investigate the complaints tenants had of their housing, and see what could be done about it. In the process, she came across many troubled Latin families. She asked for someone from the hospital to go out with her to diagnose the situation and to make known to the people what services were available to them at the hospital. There was quite a bit of work to be done also in encouraging them to overcome their fears and to accept help. Because I was Spanish-speaking, I was the one who went out on this job.

Language skills are never just language skills. They usually entail at least some understanding of the culture for which the language is the medium of communication. In the following illustration, we have an example of how linguistic knowledge or ignorance affects the client-worker relationship:

> I worked for a while with a 15 year old Puerto Rican boy who was getting into trouble using drugs, not working at school, etc. In addition to this, his guidance counselor began to think that he was very crazy - perhaps even schizoprenic. An example of his strangeness that was given was that he referred to himself as "Indian" even though he was obviously Puerto Rican. My knowledge of Spanish helped me to understand and then explain that what the boy meant was that he was of the physical type called "<u>tipo indio</u>" by the Puerto Ricans. That is, that he was dark-skinned and had straight black hair. He had simply translated the Spanish literally into English, without meaning to claim hereby that he was actually an Indian, whether American or Asiatic, as the word sug-

gests to the ears of an English speaker.

This example leads rather nicely into the general question of cross-cultural knowledge and the more specific questions of psychosocial diagnosis to be discussed below.

Sex, Family and Work Roles

Most of our students, both men and women, professed a strong belief in the equality of women. Their observation that many behaviors implying inequality were not only accepted but explicitly encouraged in Puerto Rico was part of the culture shock experience. While in Puerto Rico, the women students might react with amusement, exasperation or anger, the men with (carefully disguised) pleasure and not a little performance anxiety - but on the whole, they all knew it was their job to get to know the local culture rather than to change it.

When they came back to New York, at least some students experienced a conflict between the two cultures, and the value attitudes. The acceptance (or inhibition of protest) which they practiced in Puerto Rico could not always be transferred to New York. The project field instructor noted that some students found themselves quite unable to accept the dependent woman who passively accepts her role as less than that of the man - or the man whose very self-respect depends on maintaining his supremacy over women.

Other students succeeded in holding their personal attitudes in check, applying their new cultural knowledge and even communicating some of it to fellow staff members. Here is one example:

> My knowledge of the Puerto Rican culture is so inherently involved in my treatment of Puerto Rican patients that it is difficult to partialize. I feel it probably has helped me most in knowing what not to say or do, e.g., I have had at least one joint interview with a Latin couple. On this occasion my knowledge of the general attitude toward women by Latin males alerted me to transactions between the marital pair in my interview. The husband was somewhat casual about his wife's complaints of "nervousness" and loneliness" attributing these to her being a woman and therefore more prone to such. I gently but firmly was able to point out instances in which her complaints were valid while at the same time pointing to positive areas in their relationship. While doing this I was quite aware of having to point to the husband's interest and concern in his family as evidenced by his hardworking behavior and excellent provision for his family's material needs. That was important to the man; his feeling that he could care for his family materially.

This kind of empathy also led to a more sensitive understanding of the function of social work in general:

> Because of the knowledge of the importance of parenthood to Puerto Rican women, I was able to relate to and help relieve some of the depression of a Puerto Rican woman who was a habitual aborter (a medical term for a woman who cannot carry a fetus to term). The depression was complicated by the fact that the woman's husband was a long time street junkie (also Puerto Rican) who at the time of delivery was in a State rehabilitation facility. In her role as a Puerto Rican woman, wife and mother, this lady was completely frustrated. I was able to get the State authority to discharge

the husband to outpatient after care somewhat sooner than planned, so that he could be with her during this time. Before discharge was finalized, I arranged with the State authority's Social Services Department to have him telephone daily. The patient's chronic role failure had caused her to be seriously depressed many times before and necessitated psychiatric assistance at another hospital. The social worker from the psychiatric facility was convinced that the patient was in a sado-masochistic relationship with her husband. By exploring that most Puerto Rican women of a traditional nature accepted a high degree of dependence and submissiveness to their husbands, I feel I was able to modify the social worker's diagnostic error, and to convince her that the depression was more than likely due to the lack of role fulfillment the woman experienced. It is my understanding that the lady never returned to psychiatric treatment after her husband came home and by her admission only went for companionship.

In the broad area of work roles, we had remarkably few responses through the student follow-up. A fair example is the following:

I did work with a Puerto Rican woman (single in her 40s) who wants to be more independent and go to school to learn English, but feels it is unbecoming and feels inhibited in even thinking about future plans other than staying home. We often relate to the traditional role of the Puerto Rican women and the family's closeness and pressures on her in this direction.

This conflict between traditional sex, family and work roles illustrates the problem which some Puerto Rican women encounter in New York. Ostensibly the larger Anglo society is not only more open to women, but it encourages them to take advantage of this openness. But tradition - internalized or via external pressure - works mightily to keep them in "their place".

In Puerto Rico, our students had been exposed to a broad horizon of work roles: Puerto Ricans running their own government, Puerto Ricans in positions of unquestioned authority, Puerto Ricans successful in their endeavors and proud of their success. These are not roles usually performed by clients coming to social agencies. Hence the very limited student follow-up response in this area.

We believe that in cross-cultural programs the modest goal of seeing other culture clients in ways in which one sees same-culture clients is well worth the effort. A white Anglo client is seen in a context where other Anglos have been Presidents, rich people, powerful people, creative people, and so on. If a Puerto Rican client is seen in a context where other Puerto Ricans have achieved these statuses (whether we consider such statuses desirable or not) the client may indeed be served better. For Anglos, Puerto Ricans, and probably much of mankind, the people who are successful in their work roles constitute a reference group of major importance. It is largely against such reference groups that one's success or failure is evaluated, and one's self-respect or self-hate is developed. Clients of social agencies are failures. They are social failures if poor. They are health failures if sick (especially if they are also unable to pay doctors' bills). And they may be cultural failures if they cannot negotiate the difficult balancing act of living with two cultures, as most Puerto Ricans are forced to do. And the social worker's task is to try to evaluate the client's failure against the client's own cultural norms. It seems to us that the students who participated in our project did acquire at least the most rudimentary tools for just that kind of evaluation.

Problems of Psychosocial Diagnosis

One of the meaningful outcomes of the students' cross-cultural experience was their new competence in contributing to the diagnostic process in mental health casework. Their reports from Ponce were noteworthy for a lack of observation of acute mental health problems. To be sure, they had seen a few, and inferred the existance of some more. But by and large, their barrio live-in experience had been with families whose problems were perceived and treated in the context of the larger local culture. This means, among other things, that the families had a context of organization or coherence - something very different from the disorganization of the slum families our students had read about, and something very different from the social and cultural dislocation such as that found among New York Puerto Rican social agency clients.

Their new comprehension of this context came out most clearly in their attempt to understand and communicate to fellow staff members the practices of spiritualism. Initially, both faculty and students had perceived such practices as a somewhat exotic form of folk medicine, and no doubt we were not much different from other observers in our attitude of benign condescension. However, the students did learn to see Puerto Rican spiritualism differently. They began to see it as a way for the suffering person to explain what his affliction was - in other words, as a diagnostic process. In addition, the students (chastened perhaps by their own efforts at making their treatment techniques work, and finding these efforts productive of slow progress at best) learned to appreciate the spiritualist healing techniques as a method of therapy which might be no better than some others they had been taught in the School, but which also might just possibly not be worse. Here are two illustrations:

> I came across one lady who had been labeled schizophrenic unfairly,
> I think, largely because she talked in spiritist terms about her
> difficulties and I was able to understand that.

> I was able to reach out to Puerto Rican clients mostly by working
> on a team and being able to provide information about specific
> cultural elements to the others. Specifically I remember the
> case of a woman who, frustrated by her husband's flirtations with
> other women and frequent leavings, one night dramatically stabbed
> herself in the chest with a knife. She claimed upon talking with
> one of the psychiatric residents to have felt no pain when the
> knife went in - a sign which he diagnosed to be symptomatic of
> schizophrenia. Consequently, diagnosed her as such. I referred
> him to the concept of the ataque, and guided him to materials on
> the Puerto Rican syndrome and Puerto Rican spiritualism as a form
> of therapy.

Now, the diagnostic problems involved are complex indeed. It is difficult enough to establish a plausible diagnosis within one's own culture (the resident in the last example given might have been more careful in differentiating his diagnostic statement had he dealt with an Anglo patient exhibiting fairly familiar impulsive and dissociative behavior and anesthesia). The diagnosis becomes infinitely more difficult when it is made across cultural barriers, and our students did make the first step toward meeting the challenge of cross-cultural diagnosis when dealing with espiritismo.

The problem of treatment may simply have been beyond the scope of our project, and perhaps of our understanding. What we have learned is that, in social work practice with Puerto Ricans, some techniques which are usually the province of antropologists traveling to the far corners of the earth, are practiced right on the doorsteps of our hospitals. Just possibly we should let them in.

Respect for the Others' Culture

The students' learning process clearly resulted in a new awareness of and respect for Puerto Rican culture. It was not feasible to teach them much about Puerto Rico's intellectual history, although at least some of them got quite engrossed in it especially the flowering of Puerto Rican literature and social thought which began in the 19th century. Rather, learning occurred through everyday interactions. Some students reported the results in general terms:

> I couldn't even begin to describe all the instances in which my general heightened sensitivity to Puerto Rican problems through the language and culture have enabled me to work more effectively than I would have been able to without the project experience.

> I think the Puerto Rican project helped us (or me) serve all clients better through better self-understanding. Can't limit this to Puerto Ricans. Got a feeling of the community of man despite some important surface differences. I think my main shift in attitude came in my overcoming my dopey prejudices.

Others brought back a new awareness of what it means to be a Puerto Rican in New York.

> When clients were aware (they had an informal communication network) that I had lived in Puerto Rico, that I was positive about Puerto Ricans and spoke some Spanish, they came more readily for help. It also helped my Spanish paraprofessional colleagues to have a more positive attitude about themselves and other Puerto Ricans which helped them to work more effectively. There is apparently a lot of anti-Puerto Rican feeling in New York about which I was rather unaware.

While this student's last point may seem a discovery of the obvious, it seems useful to point out that before the project experience she had managed to ignore the anti-Puerto Rican feeling which is so loudly present in New York daily life. This student's report leads us to some of the more specific ways in which the project experience was used in practice.

Knowledge of Puerto Rican "geography" (which, given the Puerto Ricans' attachment to their hometown, has deep psychological meaning for them) clearly was an asset in establishing rapport with clients:

> There have been many times when familiarity with Puerto Rican culture has helped me to convey, I believe, an atmosphere of understanding and acceptance to clients. My familiarity with the town she came from helped one lady to open up and to trust me.

> Three clients were very pleased I had lived in their country. We discussed San Juan, Ponce and Caguas in great detail and it helped future rapport tremendously.

Sometimes small things help a lot because they reflect cross-cultural awareness:

> We write important messages in Spanish and English and include Puerto Rican recipes in the program's newspaper. While I was editor, I approached the Puerto Rican patients for their favorite recipes and included some of my own which I had collected in Puerto Rico. People later did a lot of commenting about this and seemed to appreciate it.

Many customs which seem exotic to the Anglo, perhaps at best the proper subject matter for anthropological inquiry, were now familiar to the students who could place them in the context of values to which they belong. Here is one example:

> In a group meeting that I was running one time, one of the members accused one of the others of not really loving her dead father because she never put out a fresh glass of water. The accused replied that she did, and insisted that she changed it regularly. Without having to ask, I knew that to some Latin people putting a glass of water in front of a picture of the deceased relative is an important part of the honor paid them in mourning.

More generalized value orientations were also recognized by the students and introduced into their practice:

> There have been some racial tensions in the program and I have continued to remind people of the issues of honor and respect in the Puerto Rican culture as they touched on concrete issues.

We are not suggesting that the students brought back the kind of knowledge which unfailingly alerts them to cross-cultural cues. This should not be expected from our project or any other. Cross-cultural misunderstandings occur in social work all the time, and the attempt to understand them is as old as social work itself. The project field instructor found herself exasperated at times when students failed to use their newly acquired skills. To give only one example:

> A student who, upon her return from Puerto Rico, was given the task of involving Puerto Rican parents in a local school PTA, and who held group meetings to further that purpose, called upon a group member to speak by saying: "Hey, you!" Now this was a gross violation of all the norms the student had learned. The parent in question should have been addressed formally as "Doña X", and politely requested to give her point of view - which might have carried that much more weight with the group because of the formality and politeness involved. Some people reacted sharply to this violation. Others, however, felt that it was more an expression of the existing conflict between two modes of communication which co-exist in the New York experienced by Puerto Ricans; the formal one to which older Puerto Ricans adhere, and the rather informal one which is frequently found among Anglos, and noted with surprise and sometimes disapproval by foreigners.

The project field instructor's analysis of her observations has important implications for social work practice. There is a long tradition of defining the hard-to-reach client as "resistant to treatment". This may not always be ture:

> We experienced a new view of resistance. Whereas classically resistance is defined as negative, usually a hindrance to the social work process, we found that resistance may be the quickest way a client has to let the worker know that something is clashing in the treatment process. We found cultural values to be often at the source of conflict with Puerto Rican clients, generating strong resistance. In pursuing this, we have been able to explore the nature of resistance due to cultural value clashes between client and worker, and to realize that if the treatment is to be successful, resistance must be viewed differently by the worker.

In our project, we found that looking at resistance as a positive
element facilitated worker and client positive attitudes.

We believe that this thought should be used as a starting point for further and system-
atic exploration.

Footnotes:

1. Some of the students' reactions upon their return to New York are explored in more detail in S. Pfannkuche, et. al., Los Extranjeros, unpublished M.S.W. thesis, Hunter College School of Social Work, 1972, p. 52-56.

CHAPTER 15

RECOMMENDATIONS

The project upon which this report is based sought to prepare graduate students of social work for employment serving New York City's Hispanic population. The efforts were specific and limited to social work trainees. However, our experience suggests some generalizations about learning not limited to social work, but, of a broader order, useful for those preparing to work with persons of another culture, and for those who wish to work with Hispanics in particular.

Our recommendations divide into two general areas. First, what training do social workers and other professionals need in order to enhance their ability to work with people of another country? Second, what might institutions and service systems do to make themselves more effective in dealing with such clients?

Components of a Training Program

1. For cognitive learning, the development of an appropriate knowledge base includes such basic items as language, history and culture, information about the group's current socio-economic status, migration history, some of its homeland's geography, group customs, traditions and expected behaviors.

Language must be accorded the highest priority. Knowledge of the language is obviously necessary for basic communication, and in this context, the project generated considerable evidence that even minimal and faulty language skill upgraded the ability of the social worker to function professionally to an extent beyond our expectations. In addition, language is essential for understanding of the culture of a group. Behavior is experienced largely through language, and the understanding of behavior is enchanced by the understanding of language.

With respect to knowledge about Puerto Ricans' cultural pattern and demographics, the matter is complicated by the fact that there is no single group or Puerto Rican people that social workers will come into contact with. The migration has been in process now for many years, so that different issues must be considered if professionals are to be effective.

There is a need to teach about the three different Puerto Rican groups in New York:

1. Newly arrived group; Spanish-speaking and Island centered.
2. The transitional group; bilingual and educated in New York.
3. Second generation; non-Spanish speaking.

Hidalgo refers to the new phenomenon where we need to recognize the third generation Puerto Ricans who are individually and collectively trying to recapture their "Puertoricanness".1

2. On an affective level, an acceptance of others' belief systems and social requirements, with recognition of which are functions of the group, and therefore normative, and which are functions of individual differences, and therefore idiosyncratic, is central. This means more than acceptance of the legitimacy of other cultures and their norms or individualization and the acceptance of the individual in his

own right. It suggests acceptance of the individual with recognition of the cultural context from which he comes, with more attention to cultural determinants and normative behavior. A great asset is an active curiosity about the customs of others and a positive interest in their particular rules of behavior.

Emelicia Mizio in "White Worker-Minority Client" says that common background of social worker and client is less important than many claim and that special training can help compensate for differences between worker and client.

Garcia[3] lists three major areas with which the social worker who works with a cultural group ought to be familiar. One is lifestyle, which includes attitudes about the man and his position, what it does to him to have his wife make decisions or have a female social worker advise him on family matters. The extended family patterns of the Chicano, which are similar to those of the Puerto Rican, have relevance to the fact that when workers suggest out of home placement for elderly or disabled relatives, they are violating some of the ethical and cultural standards of the family. The second area is religion. Since Catholicism is the dominant religion of the Chicano, as it is of the Puerto Rican family, the worker needs to understand the particular client in terms of his relationship with the Church, and to understand attitude toward contraceptives, abortion, marriage, separation and divorce. The third area is superstition. The non-Chicano practitioner should acquaint himself with such superstitions as mal de susto, a beaviorial condition presumed to be caused by bad fright; in the Puerto Rican culture it might be the ataque and mal de ojo, the evil eye. It is important to know about the curanderos (faithhealers) whose activities include those of social worker, doctor, and priest; they are very much the same as the Puerto Rican espiritists.

Additional program content items are suggested by the various elements described in this report. However, the fundamental approach throughout such a program must be training in the understanding of a culture from the point of view of an individual.

Some Specific Suggestions for Social Work Training

To carry out the training program, many techniques can be used. The classroom, field work, readings, lectures, and research are useful. However, this project demonstrated the unique usefulness of the experiential component we refer to as "total immersion". In this case, it consisted of barrio living in Puerto Rico. Its special character has been discussed throughout this report. The technique involves a process whereby the culture shock experienced by the students becomes a key element in the learning process. In addition, total immersion provides the strongest possible motivation for learning - survival.

This suggests some other non-traditional education patterns including opportunities for experiential learning by living with Puerto Rican families in New York City.

The training could involve two aspects:

1. For students during their regular graduate training program so that working with different cultural groups interfaces with the regular academic program.

2. For professional social workers in the field who may find themselves working in agencies where they need to serve a Puerto Rican population.

All of the recommendations that follow can be applied to full-time students; some could be more effectively used by the working professional group.

One recommendation would be to spend one academic year in Puerto Rico providing language and culture in the first semester with the second semester spent in field work in social agencies in Puerto Rico.

However, in view of some of the financial costs of residence in Puerto Rico, several alternatives are suggested for experiential learning in Puerto Rico and/or in New York.

1. Spend three months, one semester in Puerto Rico primarily for language competence; or develop language and culture program in New York City similar to program in Puerto Rico.

2. Spend one semester in Puerto Rico providing language and culture courses as well as course and field instruction at the University of Puerto Rico; or have students in New York "live-in" with families in barrios, concurrent with regular program and language course at the Hunter College School of Social Work.

3. Short-term language/culture course in Puerto Rico - 4-6 week summer package with limited language goal; or language program in the summer in New York City - 4-6 weeks.

4. Short-term - one week institutes in Puerto Rico with focus on culture (not language), plus one week preparation institute in New York City on Puerto Rican community.

5. Summer program - 12 week course in language and culture in Puerto Rico; or summer program, 8-12 weeks in language and culture in New York City.

Some Implications for Institutions and Service Systems

Certain public services are designed to provide resources and serve needs which individuals and families are unable to meet with their own resources. The public services with which we are concerned here are health and welfare services, but the remarks have equal relevance for education, police and other systems designed to serve large numbers of the public.

All newcomers to an area have problems of orientation and information. They must be introduced or introduce themselves to the new areas' customs and expectations. This kind of introduction is often carried out by relatives, friends and some voluntary groups like home town associations and other ethnic organizations.

When new arrivals speak a language different than that of the community they enter, they are immediately set apart. The use of the Spanish language in New York City is no longer conceived of as a problem of education for acculturation and proficiency in English. Bilingualism is a political and a cultural issue which is being dealt with only in part by the educational system.

If some of them have darker skin color this further separates them in a society with color biases. The color question is deeply embedded in North American society and is far from being resolved in the diffuse efforts of the major social institutions, witness the current school busing issue in Boston. Access remains limited in housing and in employment. Difference is often defined by the majority as strangeness, as unacceptable, as bad (immoral), or as sick (emotionally disturbed).

Strangers who in addition are poor share in the problems of all poor in urban communities. It is for the "poor" that the major public welfare services exist, to make up for "insufficient" income, (housing, child care, work skills, employment, etc.). While these public services exist as "rights", access is controlled by a formal "means" test which officially defines what "insufficiency" means. Informally, and more subtly, access is also influenced by English language skills and color. Service personnel are neither deaf to accents and patterns or usage nor blind to color or social status. It is not suggested that such discrimination is necessarily willful or planned, but rather that it reflects the attitudes of the larger community towards outsiders, "foreigners" (even if they are legal citizens as are Puerto Ricans, they remain de facto "aliens"), persons of color, and the poor.

Some Implications For Direct Intervention With Individuals, Families and Groups

A wide variety of questions suggest themselves. If, for example, Hispanics relate themselves more to persons than to systems and help is perceived as coming from personal intervention on the part of a patron rather than from an impersonal large organization, how may this be taken into account in designing service programs so that more meaningful contact may be established? What kind of persons with what kind of training should be employed in Intake and Admission Services? Is there a place for client (patient) advocates within the service system? (Some hospitals are experimenting with patient advocates.) What functions could they fill? At what staff level should they function? How should they be trained? Where should they be located within the service system structure? Can a large operating service organization be more responsive to individuals and the Hispanic concepts of respect and dignity?

For work with the individuals, families and groups who seek health or welfare services or for whom such services are sought by other systems (e.g. schools, courts, etc.) the findings of this report are particularly relevant. The gross misunderstanding of language and behavior often leads to faulty assessment of the applicants functioning and capacities. Culturally prescribed acceptable behavior within the particular group may be diagnosed as deviant and disturbed and in need of treatment or change (such instances have been described).

There is, therefore, a need to provide material for the social workers to deal with such problems as:

> In health and family problems who is the family authority? Which
> family member(s) should be consulted in relation to which kind of
> decision? What kinds of topics may be appropriately discussed with
> a father, a mother, parents, parents and children? What are culture
> appropriate role expectations among family members; in martial rela-
> tionships, in parent-child relationships, between the sexes, in rela-
> tion to rodinal position? How do all of these affect the definition
> of problems and diagnoses? What becomes appropriate treatment goals
> and modalities within these cultural constraints?

General Policy Recommendations

Service systems operate at the organization level in terms of policies, programs, and procedures, as well as in terms of direct service to the individual, family, or group. These general comments, the material reported from the literature, and the experiences of the students and faculty in the project also suggest some implications for the general organization policy level.

At the policy level, it is necessary to recruit more Hispanics who will know both language and culture and therefore will be able to communicate and to understand the cultural meaning of requests, definitions of problems, and usual solutions sought within the culture. From all indications, it remains unlikely that in the immediate future there will be a substantial increase of Puerto Rican or Ladino service personnel. In the absence of this kind of major change in personnel, a second policy recommendation is that Anglo personnel be trained in the Spanish language and oriented to the Hispanic cultures through extensive in-service training within service systems in the health and welfare fields.

A final policy recommendation is that social welfare institutions review their current procedures, organizational structure and policy guidelines in order to build into them some cognizance of the importance of the inter-cultural factor. This should include the entire gamut of organizational elements, ranging from agendas at meetings of boards of directors, through job specifications, down to appropriate language on record forms and directional signs. Basic policy decisions of this sort must be dealt with and supported at the highest levels of an organization, setting the tone for all other levels.

General Observation

It is our feeling that this project has already had an impact in the Hunter College School of Social Work on both faculty and students. It has helped them identify the special problems related to the Puerto Rican community and to drug addiction. It has suggested curriculum additions, some of which have been made and some of which will develop later. As important as any specific change, it has caused change in sensitivity to the inter-cultural factor in social work. It is our sincere hope that there will be continued efforts towards progress in this most important aspect of social work training.

Footnotes:

1. Hidalgo. Op. cit. p. 56

2. Emelicia Mizio. "White Worker-Minority Client". Social Work, Vol. 17, No. 3, (May 1972).

3. Garcia. Op. cit.

BIBLIOGRAPHY

Abad, Vincente, Juan Ramos and Elizabeth Boyce. "A Model of Delivery of Mental Health Services to Spanish-Speaking Minorities." Pre-Publication Draft. Presented at the 50th Annual Meeting of the American Orthopsychiatric Association, New York City, May 31, 1973.

Adler-Horton, Janet, et.al. A Study of Ten Puerto Rican Families. Unpublished Master's Project Report. New York: Hunter College School of Social Work. 1974.

Allport, G. W. The Nature of Prejudice (1954). New York: Doubleday; Anchor Books, 1958.

Allport, G. W. "The Open System in Personality Theory." In Modern Systems Research for the Behavioral Scientist. Ed. Walter Buckley. Chicago: Aldine, 1968.

"Anker Nombra 40 Escuelas Daran Instruccion Bilingue." El Diario, (6 Nov., 1974), p.2

Barna, L. M. "Stumbling Blocks in Interpersonal Intercultural Communications." In Readings in Intercultural Communications. Ed. David Hoopes. Pittsburgh: University of Pittsburgh, 1970.

Berle, B. Eighty Puerto Rican Families in New York City. New York: Columbia University Press, 1959.

Bonilla, Seda. Requiem por una cultura. Rio Piedras, P.R.: Editorial Edie, 1970.

Bram, Joseph, "The Lower Status Puerto Rican Family." New York: Mobilization for Youth, March, 1963. World of Education: School and Community Course. (Unpublished)

Bruner, Jerome S. Toward a Theory of Instruction. Cambridge, Mass.: Harvard University Press, 1966.

Cabrera, F. M. Historia de la Literature Puertorriqueña. Rio Piedras, P.R.: Editorial Cultural, 1969.

Camarillo, Mateo & Antonio Del Buono. "Utilizing Barrio Expertise in Social Work Education." In La Causa Chicana: The Movement for Justice. Ed. Margaret Mangold. New York: Family Service Association of America, 1972.

Churchman, C. West. The Systems Approach. New York: Delta, 1968.

Cole, Michael, et. al. The Cultural Context of Learning and Thinking. An Exploration in Experimental Anthropology. New York: Basic Books, Inc. 1971.

Council on Social Work Education. The Puerto Rican People: A Selected Bibliography for Use in Social Work Education. New York: Council on Social Work Education, 1973.

Cruz, Hernandez. "Cocaine Galore 1." In Puerto Rican Poets/Los Poetas Puertorriqueños. Eds. Alfredo Matilla and Juan A. Silén. New York: Bantam Books, 1972.

de Rodríguez, Ligia Vázquez. "Social Work Practice in Puerto Rico." Social Work. (March, 1973), 32-40.

Deutsch, Car. W. "Towards a Cybernetic Model of a Man in Society." In Modern Systems Research for the Behavioral Scientist. Ed. Walter Buckley. Chicago; Aldine, 1968.

Dohrenwend, B. P. and B. S. Dohrenwend. Social Status and Psychological Disorder. New York: Wiley-Interscience, 1969.

Economic Development and the Puerto Rican New Yorker. New York: Puerto Rican Forum.

Figueroa, J. A. "East 110th Street". In East 110th Street. Detroit: Broadside Press, 1973.

Figueroa, J. A. "111 Literate Poem". In East 110th Street. Detroit: Broadside Press, 1973.

Fitzpatrick, J. G. Puerto Rican Americans: The Meaning of Migration to the Mainland. Englewood Cliffs, N. J.: Prentice-Hall, 1971.

Fitzpatrick, Joseph and Robert E. Gould. "Mental Illness Among Puerto Ricans in New York: Cultural Conditions or Intercultural Misunderstanding?" Chevy Chase, Md.: Joint Commission on Mental Health for Children.

Foster, R. J. Examples of Cross Cultural Problems Encountered by Americans Working Overseas: An Instructor's Handbook. HUMRRO, 1965.

Frankel, Viktor. Man's Search for Meaning. New York: Washington Square Press, 1963.

Garcia, Alejandro. "The Chicano and Social Work." In La Causa Chicana: The Movement for Justice. Ed. Margaret M. Mangold. New York: Family Service Association of America 1972.

Garcia, C. Study of the Initial Involvement in the Social Services by the Puerto Rican Migrants in Philadelphia. Philadelphia: Vantage Press, 1971

Garrison, Vivian. "Espiritismo: Implications for Provision of Mental Health Services to Puerto Rican Populations." Pre-Publication Draft. Presented at the Eighth Annual Meeting of the Southern Anthropological Society, Columbia, Missouri, Feb. 24-26, 1972.

Giordano, Joseph. Ethnicity and Mental Health. National Project on Ethnic America of the American Jewish Committee. New York: Institute of Human Relations, 1973.

Glazer, N. and D. Moynihan. Beyond the Melting Pot. Cambridge, Mass.: M.I.T. Press 1963

Goldberg, G. S. and E. W. Gordon. "La Vida" Whose Life?" IRCD Bulletin, Vol. 4, No. 1. (1968).

Goldstein, Richard. "The Big Mango". New York, Vol. 5, No. 32 (7 Aug., 1972) 24-26.

Gould, Julius and William L. Kolb, eds. A Dictionary of the Social Sciences. New York: The Free Press, 1964.

Graham, Hugh and Ted R. Gurr. The History of Violence in America. New York: Bantam Books, 1969.

Green, H. B. "Comparison of Nurturance and Independence Training in Jamaica and Puerto Rico, with Consideration of the Resulting Personality Structure and Transplanted

Social Patterns." <u>Journal of Social Psychiatry</u>, Vol. 51 (1960), 27-63.

Greenspan, Richard. <u>Analysis of Puerto Rican and Black Employment in New York City Schools</u>. New York: Puerto Rican Forum, 1970.

Guzzetta, Charles. "Curriculum Alternatives." <u>Journal of Education for Social Work</u>, Vol. 8, No. 7 (Winter, 1972).

Hall, E. T. <u>The Silent Language</u>. New York: Doubleday, 1959.

Handlin, Oscar. <u>The Newcomers</u>. Cambridge, Mass.: Harvard University Press, 1959.

Hapgood, H. <u>The Spirit of the Ghetto</u> (1902). New York: Schocken, 1966.

Harrington, M. <u>The Other America</u>. New York: Macmillan, 1963.

Hidalgo, Hilda. "The Puerto Rican". <u>Ethnic Differences Series</u>. Washington, D.C.: National Rehabilitation Association, 1973.

Hilgard, Ernest and G. H. Bowers. <u>Theories of Learning</u>. 3rd edition. New York: Appleton-Century-Crofts, 1966.

Hill, Reuben. "Courtship in Puerto Rico: An Institution in Transition". <u>Marriage and Family Living</u>, Vol. 18 (Feb.1955).

Hofstadter, R. <u>Social Darwinism in American Thought</u>. Revised edition. Boston: Beacon Press, 1955.

Jones, M.M. Villa Flores: <u>A Community's Attitudes Toward Welfare</u>. Unpublished M.S.W. Thesis. New York: Hunter College School of Social Work, 1973.

Knowles, Malcolm S. "Innovations in Teaching Styles and Approaches Based on Adult Learning." <u>Journal of Education for Social Work</u>, Vol. 8, No. 2 (Spring, 1972).

Kolodny, Ralph. "Ethnic Cleavages in the United States." <u>Social Work</u>, Vol. XIV (January, 1969).

<u>Labor Force Experience of the Puerto Rican Worker</u>. In <u>Regional Reports</u>, No. 9 (June, 1968). (New York: U.S. Department of Labor: Bureau of Labor Statistics).

Landy, David. <u>Tropical Childhood: Cultural Transmission and Learning in a Rural Puerto Rican Village</u>. Chapel Hill, N.C.: University of North Carolina Press, 1959.

Levine, Robert A. <u>Culture, Behavior and Personality</u>. Chicago: Aldine, 1973.

Lewis, Oscar. <u>Freedom and Power in the Caribbean</u>. New York: Monthly Review Press, 1964.

Lewis, Oscar. <u>A Study of a Slum Culture</u>. New York: Random House, 1970.

Lewis, Oscar. <u>La Vida: A Puerto Rican Family in the Culture of Poverty San Juan and New York</u>. New York: Random House, 1966. Also published in New York by Vintage Books, 1965.

Luciano, Felipe. "Message to a dope fiend." In <u>Puerto Rican Poets/Los Poetas Puertorriqueños</u>. Eds. Alfredo Matilla and Juan A. Silén. New York: Bantam Books, 1972.

Maldonado-Denis, Manuel. Puerto Rico: A Socio-Historic Interpretation. New York: Vintage Books, 1972.

Malzberg, B. "Mental Disease Among Puerto Ricans in New York City, 1949-51." Journal of Nervous and Mental Disease, Vol. 123 (1956), 457-65.

Marina-Fernandez, R. "The Puerto Rican Syndrome: Its Dynamics and Cultural Determinants." Psychiatry, Vol. 24 (1961), 79-82.

Marqués, René. La Carreta (The Ox Cart) (1951). Rio Piedras, P.R.: Editorial Cultural, 1963.

Méndez, Fernández, ed. Portrait of a Society. Rio Piedras, P.R.: University of Puerto Rico Press, 1972.

Meyers, George C. and George Masnick. "The Migration Experience of New York Puerto Ricans: A Perspective on Return." International Migration Review, (Spring, 1968).

Mills, C. W., C. Senior and R. Goldsen. The Puerto Rican Journey. New York: Russell and Russell, 1967. Also published in New York by Harper, 1950.

Mintz, S. W. "Puerto Rican Emigration: A Threefold Comparison." Social and Economic Studies, Vol. 4, No. 4 (December, 1955).

Mintz, Sidney. "Puerto Rico: An Essay on the Definition of National Culture." In The Puerto Rican Experience. Ed. F. Codasco and E. Bucchioni (Eds.), New Jersey: Littlefield, Adams and Co., 1973.

Minuchin, S. et. al. Families in the Slums. New York: Basic Books, 1967.

Miranda, Magdalena, ed. Puerto Rican Task Force Report. New York: Council on Social Work Education, 1973.

Mizio, Emelicia. "White Worker-Minority Client". Social Work, Vol. 17, No. 3 (May, 1972).

Mowrer, O. H. "The Behavior Therapies, with Special Reference to Modeling and Imitation." American Journal of Psychotherapy, Vol. 20 (1966), 439-61.

Murphy, Jane and Alexander H. Leighton. Approaches to Cross Cultural Psychiatry. Ithaca, N. Y.: Cornell University Press, 1965.

The New York Puerto Rican: Patterns of Work Experience. In Regional Reports, No. 19 (May, 1971). New York: U.S. Department of Labor: Bureau of Labor Statistics).

Oberg, Kalvero. "Cultural Shock and Problem of Adjustment to New Cultural Environments." In Readings in Intercultural Communications. Ed. D. Hoopes. Pittsburgh: University of Pittsburgh, 1972.

Opler, Marvin K. Culture and Social Psychiatry. New York: Atherton, 1967.

Padilla, Elena. Up from Puerto Rico. New York: Columbia University Press, 1958.

Pederson, Paul. The Field and Focus of Cross Cultural Counseling. Unpublished paper. University of Minnesota.

Pfannkuche, S. et. al. Los Extranjeros. Unpublished M.S.W. Thesis. New York: Hunter College School of Social Work, 1972.

Podell, Lawrence. Families on Welfare in New York City. New York: CUNY Center for the Study of Urban Problems, N.d.

Price-Williams, D. R. Cross Cultural Studies. Baltimore: Penguin, 1969.

Puerto Rico Learning Center. Training Program, Fall Semester, 1973 for Hunter College School of Social Work. Ponce, P.R.: Puerto Rico Learning Center, 1973.

Readings in Intercultural Communication, Vol. III. The Intercultural Communications Network of the Regional Council for International Education, June, 1973.

Rodríguez, Carmen F. Q. The Modern Puerto Rican Family--New Pressures on Family Life. Unpublished paper. Rio Piedras, P.R.: University of Puerto Rico, 1973.

Rogler, L. H. and August Hollingshead. Trapped: Families and Schizophrenia. New York: Wiley, 1965.

Roth, H. Call it Sleep (1934). Reprint. New York: Avon Books, 1964.

Rothman, Beulah. "Perspectives on Learning and Teaching in Continuing Education." Journal of Education for Social Work, Vol. 9, No. 2 (Spring, 1973).

Sanders, Daniel. "Educating Social Workers for the Role of Effective Change Agents in a Multi-Cultural, Pluralistic Society." Journal of Education for Social Work, Vol. 10, No. 2 (Spring, 1974).

Schnapper. "Your Actions Speak Louder." The Volunteer, (June, 1969).

Senior, C. The Puerto Ricans: Strangers, then Neighbors. Chicago: Quadrangle Books, 1965.

Sierra, C. P. Maldanado and R. D. Trent. "The Sibling Relationship in Group Psychotherapy with Puerto Rican Schizophrenics." American Journal of Psychiatry, Vol. 117 (1960), 239-43.

Somers, Mary L. "Dimensions and Dynamics of Engaging the Learner." Journal of Social Work Education, Vol. 7, No. 3 (Fall, 1971).

Soto, Pedro Juan. Spiks (1956). Rio Piedras, P.R.: Editorial Cultural, 1970.

Srole, L., et. al. Mental Health in the Metropolis. New York: McGraw-Hill, 1962.

Status of Puerto Rico: Selected Background Studies for the U.S.-Puerto Rico Commission. Washington, D.C.: Government Printing Office, 1966.

Stevens, Evelyn P. "Machismo and Marianiso." Society, Vol. 3 (Sept/Oct., 1973), 57.

Stewart, Edward C., et. al. Simulating Intercultural Communication through Role Playing. Human Resources Research Office Technical Report, May, 1969.

Stycos, J. M. Family and Fertility in Puerto Rico. New York: Columbia University Press, 1955.

Tendler, D. Social Service Needs in a Changing Community: A Study of the Use of Voluntary Social Agencies by Puerto Rican Clients. Unpublished Doctoral Dissertation. New York: New York University, 1965.

Thomas, Piri. Down These Mean Streets. New York: Knopf, 1967.

Torres, Luis Llorens. "El Patito Feo." In Puerto Rican Poets/Los Poetas Puertorriqueños. Eds. Alfredo Matilla and Suan A. Silen. New York: Bantam Books, 1972.

Tumin, Melvin and Arnold Feldman. Social Class and Social Change in Puerto Rico. Princeton, N.J.: Princeton University Press, 196.

Turner, John B. "Education for Practice with Minorities." Social Work, Vol. 17 No. 3 (May, 1972).

Tyler, Ralph et. al. "Analysis of the Purpose, Pattern, Scope and Structure of the Officer Education Program of Air University." Maxwell Air Force Base, Alabama: Officer Education Research Laboratory, Air Development Command, May 1955.

U. S. Bureau of the Census. 1970 Census of Population. Subject Reports: Puerto Ricans in the United States. PC(2)-1E, June, 1973.

Vasquez, Hector I. A Demand for Adequate Education for Puerto Ricans. New York: Puerto Rican Forum, 1971.

Vasquez, Hector I. The Plight of the Puerto Rican Worker: A Case that Merits Special Attention. New York: Puerto Rican Forum, 1970.

Vivas, José Luis. Historia de Puerto Rico. New York: Las Americas, 1960.

Von Bertalanfsky, Ludwig. "General Systems Theory: A Critical Review." In Modern Systems Research for the Behavioral Scientist. Ed. Walter Buckley. Chicago: Aldine, 1968.

Wagenheim, Karl. Puerto Rico: A Profile. New York: Praeger, 1970.

Wakefield, D. Island in the City: A World of Spanish Harlem. Boston: Houghton Mifflin, 1959.

Walsh, John E. Intercultural Education in the Community of Man. Honolulu: University Press of Hawaii, 1973.

Watzlawich, P., J. Bevan, and D. D. Jackson. Pragmatics of Human Communications. New York: Norton, 1967.

Weisman, Irving. Social Work Intervention with Drug Abusers: Cross Cultural, Cross Regional. Project funded by the National Institute of Mental Health, MH 12499, 1970.

Weisman, Irving and F. S. Fchwartz. Directory of Services for the Drug Abuser and Addict in New York City. New York: Hunter College School of Social Work and New York City Addiction Services Agency, 1972.